A Commentary On The Gospel According To Mark

Rev. Dr. John Thomas Wylie

Author's Tranquility Press
ATLANTA, GEORGIA

Copyright © 2024 by Rev. Dr. John Thomas Wylie

All rights reserved. No part of this publication may be reproduced, distributed or transmitted in any form or by any means, including photocopying, recording, or other electronic or mechanical methods, without the prior written permission of the publisher, except in the case of brief quotations embodied in critical reviews and certain other noncommercial uses permitted by copyright law. For permission requests, write to the publisher, addressed "Attention: Permissions Coordinator," at the address below.

Rev. Dr. John Thomas Wylie/Author's Tranquility Press
3800 Camp Creek Pkwy S.W. Bldg. 1400-116 #1255
Atlanta, GA 30331, USA
www.authorstranquilitypress.com

Ordering Information:
Quantity sales. Special discounts are available on quantity purchases by corporations, associations, and others. For details, contact the "Special Sales Department" at the address above.

A Commentary On The Gospel According To Mark/ Rev. Dr. John Thomas Wylie
Paperback: 978-1-964810-71-3
eBook: 978-1-964810-16-4

CONTENTS

Introduction

Mark (Mark, John, Marcus) 1
The Gospel Of Mark 2
Authorship 3
The Date And Place Of Writing 6
The Readers 8
The Characteristics 9
The Content 10

Chapter One

The Title (1:1) 14
The Preparation For Christ's Ministry (1:2-13) 14
His Forerunner (1:2-8) 14
His Baptism (1:9-11) 17
His Temptation (1:12-13) 18
Christ's Ministry In Galilee (1:14-6:30) 19
The Call Of The First Four Disciples (1:14-20) 19
The First Galilean Preaching Tour (1:21-45) 21

Chapter Two

The Development Of Official Opposition (2:1 -3:12) .. 28

Chapter Three

The Second Sabbath Controversy (3:1-6) 37
Appointment Of The Twelve (3:13-19) 39
Concern Of Christ's Friends, And Accusations Of His Enemies (3:20-35) 42

Chapter Four
The Parables By The Seaside (4:1-34)............................48
The Trip To Gadara (4:35-5:20).....................................56

Chapter Five
The Gadarenes: A Demon Possessed Man (5:1-20).....59
The Woman With A Hemorrhage (5:21-43)................64

Chapter Six
Another Galilean Preaching Tour (6:1-30)....................72
Christ's Withdrawals From Galilee (6:31-9:50)...........80
Withdrawal To The Eastern Shore Of The Lake (6:31-56) 81

Chapter Seven
Discussion Of The Unwarranted Exaltation Of Tradition (7:1-23)..88
Withdrawal To The Region Of Tyre And Sidon (7:24-30) 93
Withdrawal To Decapolis (7:31-8:9) 95

Chapter Eight
The Feeding Of The Four Thousand (8:1-9)..................99
Withdrawal To Caesarea Philippi (8:10-9:50) 100

Chapter Nine
Conclusion Of Discourse (9:1-50) 110

Chapter Ten
Christ's Ministry In Perea (10:1-52) 124
Discussions Of Divorce, Children, And Wealth (10:1-31) 124
Conversation On The Way To Jerusalem (10:32-45) 132
The Healing Of Blind Bartimaeus (10:46-52) 135

Chapter Eleven

Christ's Concluding Ministry In Jerusalem (11:1-13:37) 140

The Entrance Into Jerusalem And The Temple (11:1-26) 140

The Final Controversies With The Jewish Leaders (11:27-12:44) 147

Chapter Twelve

Jesus Speaks To Them By Parables (12:1-44) 150

Chapter Thirteen

The Olivet Apocalypse (13:1-37) 162

Chapter Fourteen

Christ's Passion And Resurrection (14:1-16:20) 175

Treachery And Devotion (14:1-11) 175

The Lord's Passion (14:12-15:47) 178

Chapter Fifteen

The Lord's Passion Continued (15:1-47) 196

Chapter Sixteen

The Lord's Resurrection (16:1-20) 210

A Textual Note (16:9-20) 213

The Final Summary (16:19-20) 216

Bibliography 218

About The Author 222

About The Book 225

Introduction

Mark
(Mark, John, Marcus)

The son of Mary, a woman of Jerusalem, and friend of Paul and Barnabas. He was additionally the creator (author) of the second Gospel (Acts 12:12,25; 13:13). It is by and large concurred that he is indistinguishable from the Mark said in the epistles. John Mark is associated with leaving the missionary party at Perga.

This made Paul and Barnabas isolated on the second teacher trip, on the grounds that Barnabas needed John Mark as a friend and Paul did not (Acts 15:36-40). Later, Paul praised Mark to the congregation at Colosse, saying that Mark had been a solace to him (Col. 4:10, 11). Peter calls him "Marcus, my son" (I Peter 5:13) (The New Combined Bible Dictionary And Concordance, 1984).

The Gospel Of Mark

It is the second book in the New Testament and was written between 56 and 65 A.D. Mark primarily portrays the actions of Jesus and not his discourses. It is supposed by many that the author is the same as "Marcus" in I Peter 5:13, but whether he is the same as John Mark (Acts 15:37-39; Col. 4:10; II Tim. 4:11), is not certain. The old tradition states that Mark wrote this Gospel at Peter's request or dictation (Papias, Irennaeus). The Gospel may have been written in Rome, due to a few Latianisms in the book. He explains the Jewish phrase "defiled hands" by saying, "that is, unwashen hands."

However, it seems clear that the author was a Jewish Christian, for he was familiar with Jewish customs and he knew Aramaic. The material of the narrative is arranged in an order which not only follows the recognized general development of Jesus' ministry, but is quite chronological in its sequence of individual events (The New Combined Bible Dictionary And Concordance, 1984).

Authorship

In spite of the fact that the Gospel of Mark in itself is unknown, adequate proof is accessible to give positive, recognizable proof of the creator. All accessible declaration from the early Church Fathers names Mark, the attendant of Peter, as the essayist of the book.

The convention concerning the Marcan initiation backpedals to Papias toward the finish of the primary (first) century or ahead of schedule in the second, and it is affirmed in the compositions of such men as Irenaeus, Clement of Alexandria, Origen, and Jerome, and additionally in the second century Anti-Marcionite Prologue. That Mark, the friend of Peter, was the John Mark of Acts 12:12,25; 15:37-39 is not specifically expressed, but rather, this has been the agreement among everything except the more radical commentators.

Such ID is made by Vincent Taylor (The Gospel According to Mark, Harvie Barnscomb, The Gospel of Mark, and H. B. Swete, The Gospel According to Mark). The proof from the Gospel itself is in concurrence with the verifiable declaration of the early church. Clearly the creator knew about Palestine and Jerusalem specifically. He makes geological references which are right in fine detail (11:1), in this way noteworthy his own insight into the zone.

He knows Aramaic, the dialect of Palestine, as is shown by his utilization of Aramaic words (5:41; 7:34) and also by the proof of Aramaic impact on his Greek. That he was acquainted with Jewish organizations and traditions is to be found in the recognition with which he alludes to such things (1:21; 2:14,16; 7:2-4). These qualities all indicate that a Palestinian Jew is a creator; as per Acts 12:12, John Mark fits the portrayal since his house was in Jerusalem.

Moreover, there are signs in the New Testament that Mark and the Apostle Peter maintained a cozy relationship with each other. It has been noticed that there is a striking likeness between the general framework of Mark's Gospel and the sermon layout of Peter in Caesarea (Acts 10:34-43), which may indicate Peter as the fundamental hotspot for Mark's material. To this might be added Peter's reference to Mark as his son (I Pet. 5:13).

Upon the premise in this manner of both outside and inner proof, it is conceivable to confirm unquestionably that John Mark, the child of Mary, and the specialist of Paul and Peter, was the creator of the second Gospel. We initially know about the man Mark in Acts 12:12 regarding a supplication meeting in his mom's home.

As a young fellow, he went with Paul and Barnabas to the extent of Perga on their first missionary visit (Acts 13:5,13). Since he didn't proceed with the gathering, however, when he returned home, Paul declined to take him on his second excursion (Acts 15:35-41). Rather, Mark went with his cousin Barnabas (Col. 4:10, ASV) to the island of Cyprus. Considerably later, he showed up with Paul amid his first Roman detainment (Col. 4:10; Phm. 23,24). He was with Peter in Babylon (I Pet. 5:13), and Paul, amid his second imprisonment, asked for Timothy to convey

Mark to Rome since he had shown himself to be valuable in the work (II Tim. 4:11).

The Date And Place Of Writing

There is no express explanation in the Gospel itself, nor in whatever is left of the New Testament, from which we may find out a particular date for the cause of the book. Lately, the dominant part of researchers have set it somewhere close to A.D. 50 and 80, with the dominance of assessment favoring A.D. 65-70.

Our best reason for dating is the data from the Church Fathers. Irenaeus says, "Matthew likewise issued a composed Gospel among the Hebrews in their own vernacular, while Peter and Paul were lecturing at Rome and establishing the frameworks of the congregation.

After their flight, Mark, Peter's supporter and mediator, likewise handed down to us what Peter had lectured about. The word exodon, here interpreted as "flight," is utilized as a part of Lk. 9:31, where it is rendered as "perish" (A.V.), alluding to our Lord's demise. The

Apostle Peter additionally utilizes the word to insinuate his own particular move toward death (II Pet. 1:15).

That Irenaeus was setting the composition of Mark after the demise of Peter and Paul is authenticated by the Anti-Marcionite Prologue, which evidently declares, "After the passing of Peter himself, he recorded this same gospel ...." Such confirmation would appear to require a date after A.D. 67, the plausible year of Paul's affliction.

Then again, the way that the forecast of Jerusalem's annihilation (Mk. 13) is not put forward as satisfied may indicate a date preceding A.D. 70. The most conceivable date, in this way, would appear to be 67-70.

In spite of the fact that Chrysostom set the root of the Gospel in Egypt, there is exceptional motivation to search for its origin in the city of Rome. That such is the situation is expressly expressed by the Anti-Marcionite Prologue and Clement of Alexandria and inferred by Irenaeus.

The Readers

It has been a practically consistent supposition that the Second Gospel was coordinated with the Roman personality. The Marcan propensity for clarifying Jewish terms and traditions indicates Gentile perusers (5:41;7:2-4,11,34). The announcements of Clement of Alexandria such that those in Rome who heard Peter lecture demanded that Mark furnish them with a composed record are adequate reasons for trusting that the Gospel was penned for Roman Christians.

That the readers were Romans might be borne out by the nearness of certain Latinisms happening in the book. That they were Christians is additionally affirmed by the prologue to the Gospel, in which earlier comprehension with respect to the perusers is accepted.

John the Baptist is presented with no endeavor at recognizable proof; his detainment is alluded to as if the perusers were at that point comfortable with reality; the terms sanctify through water (1:4) and Holy Ghost (1:8) are utilized with no clarification.

The Characteristics

A few striking idiosyncrasies (striking peculiarities) of Mark's record make it interesting among the Gospels. The way of composing has been portrayed as realistic, intense, and sensational. A clear authenticity describes both Mark's style and his unvarnished announcing of the certainties.

Occasions are depicted without change or broad translation, and their introduction is set apart by an "on-the-spot" quality found in the reports of observers. A stamped power and a note of direness might be detected in any segment of the written work.

The trademark expression of this Gospel of activity is euthys, which happens somewhere in the range of forty-one times and is deciphered straightway, promptly, forthwith, anon. Greek tenses are utilized successfully to expand the sensational and realistic impact of a biography that is as of now emotional by prudence of its characteristic nature.

In various spots expressions of strange forcefulness show up, for example, "driveth' (1:12), contrasted and "drove," which shows up in the other Synoptic Gospels (Matt. 4:1; Lk. 4:1). In concordance with these idiosyncrasies is simply the curtness of the book and the compact reports of individual occasions (cf. Mk. 1:12,13; Matt. 4:1-11).

The Content

The Gospel starts with a concise record of occasions that opened people in general service of our Lord, particularly his submersion and enticement. A check has along these lines discarded, by configuration obviously, any record of the birth and initial thirty years of Christ's life.

He additionally makes no reference to the early service in Judea, which is recorded in Jn. 2:13-4:3. With no clarification of the interceding occasions, the creator moves from the allurement to the Galilean service. The main time of the work in northern Palestine was set apart by gigantic accomplishment as a group rushed to hear the new educator, with the outcome that he thought that it was important to confine the social events to the nation regions (Mk. 1:45).

Individuals originated from Judea and Idumea toward the south, from Perea toward the east, and from Tire and Sidon toward the north (3:7,8). Simultaneously, our Gospel records the beginnings of a threatening vibe to Christ with respect to the Jewish pioneers. This restriction strengthened until it wound up plainly one of the central attributes of the second time of the work in Galilee.

Accordingly, of the animosity of these pioneers and the superstitious doubts of Herod Antipas, Jesus started a progression of methodical retirements from the locale of Galilee, continually staying in the general region and frequently coming back to Capernaum for a short remain.

Amid nowadays, his fundamental occupation is the preparation of the devotees. The hour toward which he had been deliberately moving was quickly drawing nearer, and it was now that he started to set up his own by rehashed clarifications for the culmination of his natural work in his demise and restoration.

Taking after the withdrawals for devotee preparation, Mark follows Christ's last excursion to Jerusalem by method for Perea. In this manner, our creator has again excluded a sizable square of material. He has gone by the whole later Judean service and most of the work past Jordan in Perea.

With regards to the trademark curtness of the Evangelist, he moves quickly into a record of Passion Week. To this brief period, Mark dedicates very nearly six of his sixteen sections, an extent which is completely defended when one realizes this is the purposed culmination toward which the life of our Lord had been moving.

Chapter One

The Title (1:1)

These words remain as a title, showing the substance of the book in general. The "gospel" here is not the book but rather the message, the uplifting news of salvation through Jesus Christ. The truths of the life and passing of Christ make up "the start of the gospel," which suggests that the biblical lecturing was the continuation. "The Son of God." To Mark, no, not exactly to John, the divinity of Christ is of prime significance, and therefore, he incorporates it in the title of his Gospel.

The Preparation For Christ's Ministry (1:2-13)

His Forerunner (1:2-8)

Going by the birth and early years of Christ's life, Mark turns on the double to the opening occasions of the Lord's open service. As anticipated in the OT, Jesus was gone before by an envoy sent to get ready men for his appearance. John the Baptist came as the last illustrative of the old request with the express reason for presenting the key identity of the new.

2. "As it is composed." This statement is to be associated with verse 4. John's absolution and lecturing were as per the Scriptures. This was an equation used to assign "an unalterable contract." In the Prophets. The reference here is most likely a mixing of Mal. 3:1 and Exod. 23:20.

3. This bit of the citation is a practically correct propagation of the LXX perusing Isa. 40:3.

4. "Baptize" intends to plunge or submerge and in this way, alludes to a drenching. This was not a completely new ritual since Jewish convert absolution was a type of self-drenching (Moore, G.F.,1997).

John proclaimed the "baptism of repentance," which is an immersion described by and implies repentance. In the NT repentance has a more profound implication than its unique feeling of a change of psyche (change of mind). It has come to allude to an inward alter of course and reason, a turning from transgression to exemplary nature (an essential for submersion).

2. "For the remission of sins." The Greek relational word is now and again utilized with the signifying "in view of." Hence, the significance might be that John was immersed as a result of the forgiveness of sins.

5. Talking in metaphor, Mark delineates the throngs that spilled out from all parts of Judea. "There went out." The imperfect tense depicts in the movie design the consistent parade of individuals to be "purified through water" (likewise imperfect tense). The ceremony was performed "in the river of Jordan," an expression which is to be taken literally.

7-8. In verse 7,8, Mark records the center of the Baptist's message. He "preaches," or proclaimed as a herald (kerysso), the reality of the coming One. "Latchet." The cowhide strap is used to secure shoes. John did not see himself as qualified to go to the Messiah, even as an enslaved person.

8. The pouring out of "the Holy Ghost" was required to be an element of Messianic circumstances (Joel 2:28,29; Acts 1:5; 2:4,16-21). The entire age between Christ's first and second advents is viewed as being Messianic, set marked by the ministry of the Spirit.

His Baptism (1:9-11)

The high point in the service of the forerunner came when the "one mightier" than he touched base to submit to submersion (baptism). This demonstration denoted the official opening of Jesus' open service (public ministry).

9. "In Jordan." The Greek relational word "eis" signifying, "in," and "into," alongside the words, "coming up out of the water" (v. 10), show a passageway into the river suggestive of submersion. In reply to the question of why the blameless Christ was baptized with the baptism of repentance, attention ought to be paid to this deliberate demonstration of identifying with sinners. Besides, he was in full sensitivity for John's service, and to be baptized was the best thing to do (Matt. 3:15).

10. Watch the main event of Mark's trademark "straightway" (euthys); see Introduction, Characteristics. Mark's statement interpreted as "opened" is considerably more forceful in the first, intending to tear, rip in two, and render asunder. "The Spirit." Cf. Isaiah 61:1; Acts 10:38.

His Temptation (1:12-13)

Mark, in a concise summary, records the enticement (temptation) of Christ in two verses, though Matthew and Luke utilize eleven and thirteen verses separately. It is fitting that the ministry of the Savior starts along these lines. He additionally manifests his solidarity with humankind by submitting to the allurements " common to man" (I Cor. 10:13).

12. "Instantly," Same word rendered "straightway" in 1:10. "spirit," dependably not promoted in the AV, alludes to the Holy Spirit as in 1:8,10. The temptation of Jesus was no unavoidable mischance. Mark's mighty style is to be seen in "driveth," while alternate Gospels are "led."

13. See areas in Matthew 4:1-11 and Luke 4:1-3 for subtle elements of the temptations. This was an authentic enticement which Christ discovered important to oppose might be found from Hew. 2:18; 4:15. It was a reality, not a sham, and by methods for its horrendous reality Christ ended up plainly fit the bill to be our High Priest and our Example in times of temptation. That he would not respect the temper's request was guaranteed by the supremacy of his heavenly will.

Christ's Ministry In Galilee (1:14-6:30)

The Call Of The First Four Disciples (1:14-20)

Again Mark discards a segment of the life and work of Christ as he moves straightforwardly from the enticement (temptation) to the start of the Galilean ministry. After an initial introduction (vv. 14,15), he relates the call of the four fishermen to discipleship.

14. "After that, John was placed in jail." These words propose that Mark deliberately

disregarded various occasions. See John 1:35-4:42. "The gospel....of God." Manuscript confirmation is unequivocally for the exclusion of the words "of the kingdom." The message Christ continued proclaiming (kerysson, durative activity) amid the Galilean ministry was the uplifting news (Good News) that originates from God.

15. Mark includes an enhancement of the message. "The time is fulfilled." The season (kairos) of planning, the OT period, had gone to its culmination as per the arrangement of God (cf. Gal. 4:4). "The kingdom of God" alludes to the power, the illustrious rule, and the royal reign of God.

The divine sovereignty is portrayed as being "within reach," "at hand," or better, as having drawn near. It was not really present but rather conceivably so. The terms of the entrance are "atone, "repent," and.... believe the Gospel." John's was a message of repentance; however, here, another positive note is included. The kingdom in these verses is spiritual and present (cf. Jn. 3:3,5; Col. 1:13). Somewhere else,

Scripture depicts the future, eschatological kingdom.

16. "Simon and Andrew" had already turned out to be familiar with Christ as Messiah (Jn. 1:40-42). It is additionally plausible that John (Mk. 1:19) was one of those alluded to in Jn. 1:35-39 as following after Jesus.

The First Galilean Preaching Tour (1:21-45)

The Galilean ministry is set apart by three lecturing visits, in which Christ methodically conveyed his message to all aspects of Galilee. Mark accounts for the first and third of these visits. In this segment, the service in Capernaum and in the Galilean wide open is portrayed, with more prominent accentuation being set on the previous. Verses 21-34 are illustrative of one day's exercises in the ocean-side town.

21. "Capernaum" was an essential town on the primary road to Damascus, the area of a tax office, the town of the initial five disciples

whom Jesus called, and, in addition, the base camp for his Galilean service. "Taught." It was customary to welcome qualified people to educate in the synagogue.

22. "They were astonished." A compelling word, intending to hit with serious awe. "Doctrine." It was his way of instructing and the substance that astonished them in light of its distinction from the teaching of the scribes.

The last were understudies and instructors of the composed and oral law, whose way of instructing was to cite the legitimate articulations of the scribes who had gone sometime recently. Jesus talked about having direct authority from God.

24. "Let us alone." Literally, What to us and to thee? which signifies, "What have you to do with us?" The man represents himself and the devil inside. "I know thee." He knew about Christ's actual and true identity as "the Holy One of God," showing heavenly learning conferred by the evil presence.

25. "Hold thy peace." A solid word was intending to gag. The drive of the summon is

practically equivalent to our "quiet down, shut up." "Come out." Both objectives in this verse are calls for immediate consistency.

26. "Had torn him." The Spirit convulsed the man as he left him.

27. Leaving the synagogue, they went to the place of Simon, with whom Andrew, his sibling, clearly lived. "James and John" went with them, yet it is not to be comprehended that it was additionally their home. This is most likely the house alluded to in later events, which filled in as Jesus' central command (headquarters) and to which he came back from his preaching tours.

30. "Lay sick of a fever." Mark pictures Peter's relative (mother-in-law) as lying prostrate and wrecking with fever.

32. This bustling day in Capernaum was a Sabbath (v.21), which is most likely the purpose behind Mark's watchful clarification that the sick were brought "when the sunset." Healing was not to be done on the Sabbath, nor was any load to be carried.

"They brought." The Greek blemished tense implies proceeding with activity, implying that they dept on bringing them in a steady progression. "Had with demons." There is yet one fallen angel. The plural, "fiends," in the AV is to be comprehended as alluding to evil presences. Daimonizomenous signifies "devil had." Cf. 1:3439.

34. "Suffered not the devils to speak." The evil spirits were distinguishing Jesus as "Christ the Son of God" (Lk. 4:41); however, he over and over cannot (Greek, imperfect tense) give them a chance to talk. This knowledge of his person is additional confirmation that these were not just instances of (mental illness) emotional instability.

35. "An incredible while before day" alludes to the early piece of the last watch of the night, maybe in the vicinity of three and four o'clock in the morning.

His motivation was to invest energy in supplication in readiness for the proclaiming visit that was to take him into all Galilee.

39. No overstatement is proposed in the expression "all through Galilee." Instead, the aim is to supply a short synopsis of the principal Galilean preaching tour.

40. Most likely, the purifying of the untouchable, the leper (vv. 40-45) happened on the Galilean tour. "Make me clean." Leprosy brought about stately uncleanness (Lev. 13:1-3). See the leper's faith in Christ's ability.

43. "Jesus straitly charged" the man. Mark's verb conveys forceful feelings and is utilized here with extreme stern caution. It initially intended to grunt in outrage. He "sent him away," or, all the more truly, pushed him out (rejection, exebalen cf. 1:12).

44. "Say nothing.....but go." He was to go without a moment's delay to the priest and satisfy the law's prerequisites (Lev. 14:1 ff.). Until articulated clean by the priests, he had no privilege to resume his ordinary social connections.

This was to be done "for a declaration." No witness could have been more striking and legitimate than the priest's presentation of purifying and cleansing.

45. The man's inability to agree without a moment's delay added to Jesus' huge fame as a worker of supernatural miracles. Groups (crowds) were large to the point that he thought that it was important to hold the social occasions "in forsaken places," i.e., uninhabited or wild areas, desert places. What's more, "they came to him" in streams (erchonto, imperfect tense) from everywhere.

Chapter Two

The Development Of Official Opposition
(2:1 -3:12)

The motivation behind the creator in this segment is to demonstrate the improvement of contention amongst Christ and the Jewish authorities. The mushrooming prevalence of the Lord would actually stir their disapproval since his message, by its exceptional nature, was opposing to their convictions and practices.

Subsequently, in each of the five episodes recorded here, the Pharisees are seen either grumbling among themselves or transparently bringing up issues or protests.

1. This arrival (return) to Capernaum denoted the finish of the main voyage through Galilee. The expression "after some days" is best taken as alluding to the report that he had returned. Consequently, the verse ought to peruse, "And when he enters again into Capernaum, after some days it was accounted for that he was at home." The "house" was presumably Peter's (1:29), and he may well have handed off to Mark the record which takes after.

3. "Paralysis" is better comprehended as loss of motion. The man is called Paralytikon.

4. "Press." It's an old word for a crowd. As a rule, an ancient flat level roofed house had a stairway to the rooftop, which would have empowered the bearers to convey the disabled without trouble. "Revealed the rooftop." This was accomplished by burrowing through the composite of grass, mortar, tiles, and slat, as demonstrated by Mark's exoryxantes - "had broken it up" (AV). The "bed" was a sleeping cushion, a pallet, or a bed, for example, and was utilized by poor people.

7. If a man acknowledges the presumption of the recorders that Jesus was a simple man, he should arrive in like manner at their decision. He was talking "profanations." The essential clash concerned the deity of Christ.

10. "That ye may know." The recuperating of the incapacitated turned into proof of the Lord's energy to excuse sins in this manner of his divinity. "Son of man." This is the title that Jesus utilized only for himself. Its experience is to be found in Daniel and in the additional - Biblical whole-world destroying writing of the

Jews, where it had turned into an assignment of the Messiah (cf. Dan. 7:13,14).

"Power." The Greek word implies authority.

12. That he emerged "immediately" demonstrates another momentary recuperation so entirely that the man could convey his own particular bed. The outcome was that "they were altogether stunned." They were so significantly bewildered that they were close to themselves. The verb existemi signifies "to evacuate strangely, to remove out of place," or "to drive one out of one's detects."

13. The primary charge against the Lord in the arrangement of contentions recorded by Mark was the allegation of disrespect (2:1-12). A moment of protest now is brought up in 2:13-27 such that Christ related with outsiders.

14. "Levi the child Alphaeus" is the same as Matthew (Matt. 9:9, Mk. 3:18). "Receipt of custom." The duty office. Capernaum was situated out and about, driving from Mesopotamia to Egypt and close to the intersection of the interstate to Damascus. Its circumstance close to the fringe of Herod

Antipas' region clarifies the nearness there of a tollhouse.

15. "Sat at meat." The verb intends to lean back at dinner, which is the standard way of eating around then. "His home." Cf. Lk. 5:29. "Publicans." An assignment for assessment authorities. The benefit of gathering expenses was bought by installment at the aggregate tax exemption required by the administration.

The gatherer was without then to separate however much as could be expected from the general population through blackmail. Typically, the real accumulation was made by lesser authorities, of which class Matthew likely had a place. These men were loathed due to their administration of a remote overlord and their deceitful practices.

16. "The Scribes and Pharisees." The Pharisees were an order of laymen who took after thoroughly the composed and oral law statutes, being fastidious in their endeavors to keep up formal virtue. They saw with despise the individuals who were not as strict as they were in watching the rules, alluding to them as "the general population of the land" (cf. Jn. 7:49).

The class assigned as "heathens" here most likely incorporated all non-Pharisees.

17. "They that are whole." Those who are solid, strong, and healthy. Jesus was noting the pundits from their own perspective. They expected that they themselves were equitable and thus did not need assistance. Jesus talks as the doctor whose obligation it is to help the wiped out.

18. The following episode recorded by Mark is the cross-examination concerning fasting (2:18-22). "Use too fast." The Greek says essentially that they were fasting. Maybe the very time of Levi's devour was a quick day since it was the act of the Pharisees to quickly twice per week, on Mondays and Thursdays (Lk. 18:12). The way of John's service and message was in amicability with the recognition of fasting.

19. "The offspring of the bridechamber." Literally, the children (sons) of the bridechamber. These were the dear companions of the groom who filled in as his chaperons, a figure utilized here to allude to Jesus' followers. Christ came

to report happy news (cf. 1:14,15); with such a message of bliss, fasting was totally confused.

21. "New cloth." This is fabric that has not been dealt with by the more full, not contracted or measured. "Else the new piece." A nearby interpretation of the first would generally read the filling (that is, the fix) removes (tears) from it, the new from the old. At the point when the unshrunken fix winds up plainly wet, it therapists and tears far from the more established, beforehand contracted fabric. In this manner, it is not wise to endeavor to fix the old framework with the new.

22. "Old bottles." Actually, the word alludes to wineskins, which are compartments produced using the skins of creatures. The development brought about by the maturing of "new wine" would blast old wineskins since they had as of now, been extended however much as could be expected. In this way, it is impractical to limit the structure of the old legalism to the essentialness of the new experience delivered by confidence in Christ.

23. The following two events for resistance to Christ concern the Sabbath hones (2:23-3:6).

"The corn fields." Corn, our maize, was not known to the interpreters of the AV. They utilized the term as we utilize "grain." The followers were picking not "ears of corn," but rather heads of grain, for example, grain or wheat.

24. "That which is not legal." It was not the appropriating of the grain to which they questioned, for the law permitted this (Deut. 23:25); they were reprimanding physical work on the Sabbath. In their enthusiasm to keep the letter of the law to its last detail, they saw the picking of the grain as collecting and consequently as an infringement of Exod. 20:10.

25. Jesus answered by referring to "what David did" one time, as recorded in I Sam. 21:1-6. His question expects an agreed answer. The striking element of the occurrence is found in the announcement that "he had required."

Christ is proclaiming that human need supersedes all simple custom and function.

27. "The sabbath" was not expected to be an unfeeling dictator that man must serve, paying

little heed to the cost to himself; rather it was given to address man's issue for rest.

28. "Lord also of the sabbath." Christ was not affirming his opportunity to abuse the Sabbath law, rather he was pronouncing his capability to translate that law.

Chapter Three

The Second Sabbath Controversy (3:1-6)

1. The second Sabbath debate recorded by Mark (3:1-6) happened in "the synagogue," most likely in Capernaum, since 3:7 talks about a withdrawal "to the ocean."

2. The Lord's faultfinders "watched him" steadily and nearly. The verb shows a vindictive lying in hold up to trap a man. Honing pharmaceuticals on the Sabbath was prohibited by rabbinic convention unless the wiped out individual was very nearly demise, which was not valid for this situation. Thus, if Christ recuperated the man, the Jews were prepared to blame "Him" as a Sabbath violator.

4. "It is lawful." The subject of Jesus beholds back to the rule of need that had been put forward in the past Sabbath experience. To address this present man's issue would be "to do great;" to neglect to do as such would be "to do insidious." : They held their peace." The Greek flawed tense pictures them as enduring in their quiet. To answer would have been harmful. Clearly, it was not legal to do abhorrent, and to do great is to mend the man.

6. The "Herodians" were not principally a religious organization. Rather, they were men who were politically dedicated to the Herodian family. Thus, they had no genuine partiality with the Pharisees, who ardently detested outside mastery; however, a typical adversary can bring adversaries into abnormal coalitions.

7. The episode recorded in verses 7-12 gives another look at the across the board acclaim of the Lord, which conveyed individuals from far and close to observe and hear him. The group was made up of people from each segment aside from Samaria, notwithstanding including some from zones outside Palestine, for example, Tire and Sidon (vv. 7,8). "The Sea" to which "Jesus withdrew" was the Sea of Galilee.

9. "Small ship." The more exact interpretation today would be a little vessel. The group was large to the point that it was squeezing (thlibo) upon Jesus, and he was in peril of being pulverized. In this manner, the vessel was to "tend to him" altogether so that he may get into it on the off chance that it ended up noticeably important to get away from the weight of the group.

10. This awesome prominence was created on the grounds that "he had healed many." The enthusiastic longing of the debilitated and harrowed to get help is obvious in the words "they pressed upon him." Literally, they fell upon him. Stamp says, implying that they moved toward the Lord enthusiastically, basically tossing themselves upon him. The verb is durative in constraining, portraying proceeded with activity.

11. See remarks on 1:34,34.

Appointment Of The Twelve (3:13-19)

From the earliest starting point of the work in Galilee (1:14) to the decision of the twelve messengers, Jesus encountered astounding accomplishments in contacting the general population with his message. He had admittance to the synagogues, and authority resistance was just starting to cement. Nowadays, he was assembling a gathering of devotees from whom he would choose a perpetual band of pupils.

Conversely, the second time of the Galilean service was set apart by the designated colleagues. The service to the large number went on; however, there was an endeavor on Jesus' part to start his followers' direction. His prevalence with the average folks and the restriction from the pioneers kept on creating until at last, it ended up plainly essential for him to pull back from Galilee.

13. The decision of the followers happened "on a mountain," presumably in the region of Capernaum. It creates the impression that Jesus requested that a bigger gathering accompany him on the Slope Nation excursion.

14. Out of this bigger gathering, he chose "twelve," whom he named as his messengers (cf. Lk. 6:13). He was "Ordained." The Greek verb is better rendered as "named" (epoiesen; truly, he made). The motivation behind the arrangement was twofold: that they ought to be with him (for friendship and preparing), and that they may go out to lecture and to cast out evil spirits (v.15).

16. For the event when Simon was "surnamed Peter," see Jn. 1:42, where the Aramaic,

Cephais, is utilized rather than the Greek, "Peter."

17. "Boanerges." This side of their identities might be seen in Lk. 9:54.

18. "Andrew." The brother of Peter (Jn. 1:40,41). "Bartholomew." May be indistinguishable from Nathanael (Jn. 1:45-51; 21:2). "James the son of Alphaeus" might be the same as James the less (Mk. 15:40). "Thaddaeus" is additionally called Lebbaeus (Matt. 10:3) and is the same as Judas the brother of James the less (Lk. 6:16). "Simon the Canaanite" is all the more accurately assigned Simon Zelotes (Acts 1:13), or Simon the Zealot. "Canaanite" is deluding for the term found in the better Greek original copies is "Kananaion," a transliteration of an Aramaic term signifying "zealot."

Before becoming a disciple of Christ, Simon was an individual from the fanatically enthusiastic gathering of Zealots, who were agreeable to prompt rebellion against Roman overlordship.

19. It is now that Matthew and Luke put the Sermon on the Mount. "Into a house." An expression signifying "to come home." Christ most likely returned to Peter's home in Capernaum.

Concern Of Christ's Friends, And Accusations Of His Enemies (3:20-35)

These verses are characteristic of the dispositions of companions and enemies toward Jesus. Both gatherings misjudged him, with the outcome that his companions turned out to be excessively worried for his welfare, while his foes swung to horrible allegations against him.

20. "They couldn't ... eat bread." Again, Mark looks at the immense group that persistently came to hear and see Christ. "Bread" is to be comprehended as alluding to nourishment when all is said in done.

21. The "friends" who wound up plainly concerned were really individuals from Jesus' family, which is the ordinary implication of the

Greek expression, hoi standard' autou. It appears that word went to his mom and siblings in Nazareth concerning his perpetual action. Their motivation was "to lay hang on" Christ and bring him with them by drive since they felt that he was exhausted and rationally disturbed.

22. When the family landed at Capernaum, they found the Lord occupied with discussion with "the scribes ..... from Jerusalem." The recorders occasioned the exchange rehashed allegations (Gr., defective tense, elegon) that Jesus was allied with sinister power.

"Satan." The source and importance of the word are not sure, but rather, it is clearly utilized here to allude to the villain, "the sovereign" of evil presences (not "fiends;" see 1:32). The allegation was that Christ was engaged by Satan himself and that by this implies he cast out demons.

23. Jesus stepped up and "called" his accusers to come and meet him up close and personal. The rationale he utilized against these informers is unanswerable: If it is concurred that evil presences are Satan's hirelings, then it

is outlandish to affirm that he is throwing out his own particular workers. This contention the Lord repeated in 3:24-27, supporting it by a progression of representations.

27. The "strong man" is planned to speak to Satan. To cast out evil spirits is to enter his "home" and "ruin his products." Christ was declaring that as opposed to being allied with Satan, He was occupied with battle against him.

29. Blasphemy "against the Holy Ghost" is the demonstration of criticizing, censuring, and talking perniciously against the Spirit. For such a sin, there is never any "forgiveness." "In danger of." A more right interpretation would be blameworthy or bound by the feeling of being in its grip. The greater part of the better compositions read unceasing sin as opposed to "eternal damnation."

30. "Because they said." The announcements of the recorders are to be taken as uncovering the way of this everlasting offense. They clarified Christ's marvels of expulsion as being refined by otherworldly power when the Holy Spirit fashioned them as a general rule.

Notwithstanding, we are not to decipher this section as showing that the minor articulation against the Spirit is the indefensible sin, for this would be in opposition to the general instructing of Scripture that all transgressions will be excused to the humble soul.

The pith of the "interminable sin" is the state of mind of the heart that underlies the demonstration. In the light of Scripture, this disposition must be a settled, unrepentant perspective that continues in insubordination to dismiss the suggestions of the Holy Spirit.

31. While Jesus was occupied with this dialog with the copyists, "his brethren and his mother" came and were "calling him." They evidently had traveled from Nazareth to bring him home with them for the rest and recovery they accepted he required (cf. 3:20,21). "Brethren." See remarks on 6:3.

33. Christ seized upon this event as a chance to point out the significance of being profoundly identified with himself.

34. Entrance into God's family is picked up by doing "the will of God," and such compliance

starts by hearing, accepting, and taking after God's Son.

Chapter Four

The Parables By The Seaside (4:1-34)

Here is an alternate technique for instructing goes to the fore. While Christ had made utilization of illustrative education to a constrained degree already, it was not until this point in his service that he started to utilize it as a noteworthy vehicle of expression. As the group developed, resistance escalated, and as shallow devotees increased, Jesus received the illustration as a method for training his particular pupils from one perspective and disguising the substance of his instructing from shallow and adversarial listeners on the other. During this event, he utilized the stories to delineate certain attributes of the Kingdom.

1. The setting for the introduction of the first of these anecdotes was "by the seaside," which apparently alludes to the Sea of Galilee. Again, the weight of the group constrained the Lord to address the general population from a watercraft remaining off the shore for a short separation.

4. The soil "by the wayside" had been compacted by the section of numerous feet so

that the seed lay at first glance on display, and the winged animals (birds) "came and devoured it."

5-6. The second zone where the seed fell was "stony ground," which is not to be comprehended as soil containing stones but rather as a shake with a thin covering of soil. The warmth from the sun initially made this ground a hotbed, delivering fast germination and then a furnace that "scorched" and "withered" the delicate plant.

8. Furthermore, the rest of the seed was sown "on good ground." It is just sensible to expect that the colossal greater part of the seed was sown on this sort of soil and not a negligible 25 for each penny, as is now and again affirmed. "That jumped up and expanded." It was not the organic product that jumped up. These two participles allude to "other," and consequently, the seed was developing.

11. "The mystery." In the agnostic mystery religions, the start was told in the obscure educating of the clique, which was not uncovered to pariahs. On the kingdom of God, see remarks on 1:15. "The secret of the

kingdom" in its definitive advancement is the full-orbed message of the Gospel (cf. Rom. 16:25,26).

The motivation behind "parables" was to educate the stars without uncovering the things of direction to the ones who were "without."

This is with regards to the Biblical rule that otherworldly comprehension is limited to the individuals who have progressed toward becoming "spiritual" by appropriately relating themselves to Christ and his message (I Cor. 2:6 ff.).

12. That such was the motivation behind Christ's utilization of illustrations is additionally affirmed by a citation from the OT. The reference is presented with the Greek conjunction hina ("that"), which in this example can't have resultant importance; however, it should demonstrate reason. This verse is a free rendering of Isa. 6:9,10, giving the prophetic entry's substance, however, not duplicating the correct wording.

14. "The sower" (v.3) is not identified, but he clearly speaks to Christ himself and not others

who broadcast the Gospel. As Luke clarifies, the seed remains for "the word," which is the expression of God or the message that originates from God.

15. The birds of 4:4 are illustrative "of Satan," who goes to the individuals who hear the message and keep any seed germination. These people just hear the word, and that is all.

16. Cf. Verses 5,6. A few listeners to the word "receive it" with energetic willingness. The presence of truthfulness and honest-to-goodness satisfaction is available.

17. The announcement that they "have no root" shows the triviality of their gathering of the word. They "persist, however, for a period" or are brief, which is a superior interpretation of proskairoi. The warmth of the sun (v.6) delineates the happening to "torment or mistreatment," which soon turns into a stumbling block or a catch to them, and they fall away in light of the fact that their experience of the world was not honest to goodness.

19. Cf. 4:7. The considerations are nerves and stresses concerning the interests of this present underhandedness age ("world" is a wrong interpretation of aion, which alludes to a timeframe). The "deceitfulness of wealth" has reference to the beguiling way of riches, continually encouraging to fulfill but then never ready to satisfy the guarantee. The third block is the aching or desiring for "other things," a general classification including whatever else would stifle the word and make it move toward becoming "unfruitful."

20. Cf. 4:8. The great soil implies the people who "hear the word and receive it." Matt analyzes the importance of "get" in otherworldly ways. 13:23 and Lk. 8:15. These are individuals who listen, who comprehend, who are earnest, and who propel the message of the Gospel for all time.

21. The sayings of 4:41-23 are general articulations that Christ appears to have utilized in different circumstances (on v.21 cf. Matt. 5:15; on v.23 cf. Matt. 11:15; 13:9,43; Lk. 14:35; on v. 24b cf. Matt. 7:2; on v.25 cf. Matt.25:29). Christ's purpose on this event

was to stress the obligation occupant upon the listener to the stories. He who has been illuminated (enlightened should thus enlighten others (Mk. 4:21-23).

"Candle" lamp is a more exact interpretation. "Bushel." is not the same as the present-day bushed, equivalent to our peck measure. The "candle" was actually a lampstand for the open-bowl oil lights utilized as a part of that day.

25. "He that hath." The rule put forward in this announcement is to be connected particularly to the domain of truth and its assignment. He who lays hold of truth and utilizes it will get greater illumination, yet he who declines to find suitable truth will lose even the comprehension of truth that he once had.

6. The second illustration of the kingdom that Mark records is that of the dirt delivering suddenly (vv. 26-29). In all actuality, it takes up the latest relevant point of interest, going ahead to depict the real development of the seed, which proves to be fruitful. The part of "the kingdom" in view here is the present, profound viewpoint of its interior reality and

its outer indications. This kingdom is stretched out by the sowing of the "seed" of the word (cf. v.14).

28. The reason why the earth delivers "fruit of herself" (automatic, "naturally") is that the seed contains life, which, when put into the best possible condition, produces development. The normal for the present, profound kingdom of beauty, as put forward by this illustration, is that the message of the Gospel, by its extreme nature, when sown in men's souls, produces development and productivity suddenly.

30. Mark's third parable of the Kingdom concerns the mustard seed (vv. 30-32). The AV focuses on the genuine way of an anecdote by deciphering parabole as "comparison."

31. Here, the Kingdom is contrasted with a "grain of mustard seed." Much has been composed concerning the distinguishing proof of this plant. However, it appears to be best to take it to be the basic dark mustard, which has a seed about the span of the leader of a stick (Harold N. furthermore, Alma L. Moldenke, 1986). Its seed was one of the littlest known to the general population of Galilee.

32. The exceptional marvel of this specific mustard plant is that, it is truly a herb. It might develop to be ten or twelve feet high, with a stem the measure of a man's arm, and turn into a resting place for the littler assortments of winged animals.

This story further advances the qualities of the present, otherworldly kingdom of God. The primary point here is that the seed of the Gospel message will create remarkable development. From little beginnings, the Kingdom, which had just gravitated toward the individual of Christ (1:14,15), will develop to gigantic extents by reason of its own inward and heavenly imperativeness.

This does not imply that it will bring about world transformation that man by his endeavors, will acquire the kingdom of God on earth as a Utopian improvement, or that the kingdom and the Church are indistinguishable. The illustration does, be that as it may, picture the kingdom of elegance as including huge numbers of recovered people who, during that time, have come to swell its positions to phenomenal size.

The Trip To Gadara (4:35-5:20)

Presumably, for protection and unwinding, Jesus proposed a trek over the pool of Galilee. With the clarity so normal for our creator, Mark gives a realistic record of the stilling of the tempest (4:35-41) and of the liberating of the decried man whom Christ met on the opposite side (5:1-20).

37. "The Great storm of wind" was normal of the Sea of Galilee, arranged in a pocket, as it might have been, with slopes on each side. The ascending of the warm demeanor of the day permitted the cooler air from the slopes to surge down the gorges onto the lake, turning hurricane activity that agitated the waters into a furious storm. Mark's record paints a striking picture, taking his perusers to the very scene of activity. "The waves" continued beating (Gr. defective tense) into the vessel, which is now loading with water.

39. Interestingly, Mark relates the summon of Christ to the tempest. The Greek aorist tense is utilized to demonstrate that he "rebuked" it once (point activity), and the "wind ceased"

without a moment's delay, and a "quiet, calm" came promptly. The Lord did not need to repeat his charge, for it brought immediate acquiescence.

"Peace, be still." Be quiet. Be gagged. Lenski strangely deciphers the ideal tense basic of Christ's second summon, "Put the muzzle on and keep it on" (Lenski, 1951).

40. "Fearful." Christ rebuked them for their weak dread, transforming the event into a jolt of confidence. He recommended that if their certainty had been in God, despite the fact that he himself was sleeping, they would have had no motivation to fear.

41. "Feared exceedingly." Literally, they feared with great fear. The Greek expression utilized here is not the same as in verse 40. This word can signify "respectful fear or awe, reverential." Notwithstanding all the compelling works the devotees had seen, so marvelous was this supernatural occurrence that, regardless they pondered who their educator truly was. "What way of man." The Greek content has, Who then is this?

Chapter Five

The Gadarenes: A Demon Possessed Man (5:1-20)

5:1. Greek original copies are partitioned among three names here - Gadareness, Gerasenes, and Gergesenes. The best proof favors Gerasenes, a term which some have taken to allude to the notable Gerassa, twenty miles southeast of the Sea of Galilee. There is justifiable reason, be that as it may, to trust that Mark alludes to a residential area of a similar name on the eastern shore, the vestiges of which are today called Kersa (cf. Branscomb, 1952).

3. This man had his Habitual "dwelling" in or among "the tombs," as the Greek defective tense shows. He had achieved a phase so extraordinary that he could never again be bound by anybody, even "with chains."

4. The inconceivability of controlling the man is underscored drastically by clear terms and tenses. The "shackles" (fetters) were utilized on the feet. As frequently as he had been bound, he had pulled "the chains" separated and "could .... tame him." The Greek shows that

nobody had sufficient quality to tame this wild brute of a man.

5. All through "night and day," he was persistently "crying" with shouts and yells and "cutting himself" with stones. The last verb is a serious shape, implying that he was cutting himself up or slicing himself to pieces.

7. "Jesus, thou Son of the most high God." An astounding sign of supernatural knowledge. The afflicted man knew both the human name of Jesus and of his Deity, in spite of the fact that this, as it shows up, was his initial experience with Christ. Such information is evidence that the man was not just crazy; he was indwelt by satanic forces who knew the genuine recognition of Christ. "Torment me not."

Matthew 8:29 peruses, "Art thou come hither to torment us before the time? What's more, Luke 8:31 (ASV) gives additional light by announcing that they requested that he not send them "into the abyss." The torment of which the evil presences talked is the last discipline after the day of judgment; they requested that they not be detained in the pit before that time.

10. The importance of the expression "out of the country" is to be found in Luke's reference to "the abyss" (8:31, ASV). They dreaded being brought back to the place of confinement and staying in an immaterial state until the judgment.

12-13. As opposed to being disembodied, they asked to be sent "into the swine." "Jesus gave them leave (permission)." The question determinedly incited by this section concerns the moral property of Jesus' activity, coming about as it did in the devastation of the property of others.

A typical answer has been that Jews had no privilege to claim pigs, and that Christ subsequently censured their infringing upon Mosaic law. Be that as it may, since the district of Decapolis contained a blended populace of both Jews and Gentiles, we have no confirmation that the proprietors were Jews or this was the motivation behind Christ's activity.

See that he didn't order the evil spirits to enter the swine; he allowed them. The evil presence, not the Lord, brought about the annihilation. The way Christ allowed the demonstration makes him less mindful than God, who is in charge of fiendishness, since he allows it. The fallen angel's torment of Job is a valid example (Job 1:12; 2:6,7).

15. They "were afraid" not of the cured man but rather of the astounding force that had cured him. They knew about supernatural power in the individual of Christ; however, they were ignorant of his endless love, mercy, and kindness.

17. Unknowingly, they begged the source of potential blessing and salvation "to leave" out of their country. "Coasts." The Greek word implies limit, outskirts, and in the plural, it might allude to the territory surrounded by these limits (boundaries).

18. While Jesus was getting into the boat, the cured demoniac continued asking to "be with him." only he, among all his comrades, found in Jesus not someone to fear but rather someone to love.

19. "Jesus suffered him not." That is, he didn't allow the man to go with him. Rather, he instructed him to go to his own people and report to them "what awesome things (great things) the Lord hath done." An essential guideline underlies Christ's command.

Man is not delivered from bondage simply for his own delight in God-given freedom; additionally, he may offer testimony to others concerning the divine Deliverer. In the nation east of the Sea of Galilee, there was no motivation to fear any crisis brought on by excessive popularity.

In this manner, the cured demoniac was encouraged to communicate his story. "Hath had compassion." The Greek verb intends to have mercy or pity on someone.

20. "In Decapolis." This is the district southeast of the Sea of Galilee in which were found ten cities (deka, "ten"; polis, "city"). Grecian in association, organization, and culture.

The Woman With A Hemorrhage
(5:21-43)

Two momentous supernatural occurrences are depicted in the accompanying verses. The recuperating of the lady with the drain happened with no evident cognizant follow-up on Christ's part. The bringing up of the little girl of Jairus was the second example in Christ's service of the reclamation of life to the dead (cf. Lk. 7:11 ff.).

22. Jairus was "one of the leaders of the synagogue," distinguishing him as one of the older folks who were accountable for the administrations in the synagogue by Jesus at Capernaum.

23. He "besought him greatly." He continued asking, maybe over and over and urgently. "Little girl." All reporters not the minor frame as a term of charm. "At the purpose of death." A great reword of the Greek content demonstrates that she was in the last phase of her sickness. "I pray thee." These words were provided by the interpreters of the AV.

Mark's Greek distinctively depicts the anguish of this poor father as he begs broken expressions: "My little girl is passing on nearly dead - that you may come and ..."

24. The huge number after Christ continued swarming against him on each side (Gr. devil. tense, synethlibon).

25. "An issue of blood." None of the Gospels particularly depicts the way of this drain but state that it was a perpetual illness.

26. Check is extremely blunt in his remarks concerning the woman's involvement with "numerous doctors." She went to a great many doctors to be recuperated. Rather, she endured numerous things at their hands; she spent all that she had, and still she deteriorated. Luke, the doctor, is not all that is limited in his depiction (Lk. 8:43).

27. "The Press." The jam that continued squeezing in on Christ.

28. "She said." "She kept saying" (Gr. demon. tense), most likely to herself.

29-30. This recuperating was interesting, not only in light of the fact that it was immediate but rather on the grounds that it happened with no evident cognizant investment by Christ. Be that as it may, "Jesus immediately" knew about what had happened. We are not to expect that touching the article of clothing had an enchanted impact, but instead that Jesus, in omniscience, perceived the touch of faith and granted the woman's craving (desire).

Or, then again, it might be accepted that the mending was not a cognizant demonstration of Christ, and that it was God the Father who recuperated the woman. All things considered, Jesus, in the constraint of his humankind, didn't know about it until the supernatural occurrence happened. "Virtue." It was "power" (Gr., dynamin) that was an agent in the recuperating. The question "Who touched my garments?" may have been requested that all together uncover the marvel to the group, on the off chance that it be expected that the recuperating was deliberately done on Christ's part. If not, Christ may likewise have been requesting his own particular data.

31. Of course, Mark's realistic utilization of tenses is edifying. He reports that "his disciples" continued saying, "You see the crowd constantly thronging you..."

32. Apparently, the woman was not found with one look, for Mark says that he continued looking "roundabout" (indirectly) himself.

34. "Thy faith." We see this current woman's confidence (faith) in real life in 5:27,28, a certainty so solid that she didn't feel it important to capture Jesus' attention. "Made the whole.... be whole." The principal expression actually implies that she has spared you, alluding to salvation from her physical distress.

The second expression intends to be well sound and is a present goal, implying that she was to proceed in well-being.

35. The subject of the messengers, "Why troublest thou....assist?" shows that they didn't expect a restoration of life. "Master." The Greek content has didaskalon, which means "teacher."

36. Jesus, disregarding the messengers' comments, said to the ruler, "Quit dreading! Simply continue trusting!" Both verbs are of the current state in Greek. The report had struck dread into the man's heart, yet Christ asked him not to neglect his past confidence.

38. "The tumult." Among the Jews grieving for the dead, that was not stifled and conscious. Proficient grievers were employed to exhibit distress. Matthew 9:23 (ASV) notices the flute players and the group, which were additionally making a tumult.

39. The mistake of the show moved Christ to ask, "Why make ye this ado?" or, all the more truly, "Why are you making such an uproar?" Christ's announcement that the young woman was not "dead" but rather sleeping has been interpreted by some as meaning that she was not so much dead but just in a state of unconsciousness, a coma.

In any case, Lk. 8:55 says that "her spirit returned once more," showing that she had been dead. Christ's reference to death as rest was expected to recommend that the condition was transitory and that the individual would stir once more.

40. The grievers (mourners), taking Jesus' different method of expression truly, continued snickering him to "scorn." They realized that the young woman was dead, and they were certain that demise is perpetual. "Put them all out." Mark's verb is intense, which means to push out. Christ drove the sneering group from the house.

41. "Talitha cumi." Transliteration of the Aramaic for "little girl, arise." Mark embeds the words, "I say unto thee."

42. "Straightway," the young girl "arose" and was strolling around (constant activity). "Twelve years." She was mature enough to walk. The guardians and supporters were unbelievably "astonished" at the supernatural occurrence, to such an extent that they were alongside themselves with astonishment.

43. Jesus ordered "that no man ought to know" or the guardians ought to declare the news abroad and the broad fervor ought to hasten an

emergency before the hour for the Savior's demise had arrived (Jn. 12:23, 27).

Chapter Six

Another Galilean Preaching Tour *(6:1-30)*

Marks records, however, two of the Lord's three voyages through Galilee, the first with the four anglers (1:35-45) and the third at the finish of the Galilean service (6:1-30). The second visit happened not long after the decision of the Twelve (Lk. 8:1-3). The third was not the same as the first two in that the followers were conveyed two by two (Mk. 6:7), after which Christ went from town to town, lecturing and instructing without anyone else's input (Matt. 11:1).

The visit ought to include the visit to Nazareth (Mk. 6:1-6). Additionally, during this time, Herod moved toward becoming practiced concerning the immense prominence of the Lord (6:14-16).

1. "From there upon." That is, from Capernaum. While the place to which Jesus went is not particularly named, it is clear from the accompanying verses that his "own particular nation" alludes to the place where he grew up, Nazareth.

3. Jesus is called "the Brother of James" and the others, an assignment which ought to be taken truly. There is no Biblical reason for not understanding these four men and their "sisters" to be the offspring of Joseph and Mary, conceived sometime after Jesus. "James" turned into the pioneer of the Jerusalem church (Acts 15:13 ff.) and the creator of the epistle that bears his name.

"Juda" is the same as Jude, the creator of the general epistle of Jude. The townspeople "were annoyed." This verb initially signified "to be gotten in a trap or catch." They were caught in the catch of their own unbelief and staggered when they could have ascended to their most noteworthy open door.

5. Christ was not able to do any "strong work" there. Be that as it may, it was not that he attempted to recuperate a few and got himself unfit; however, so few individuals had enough confidence to come to him for mending.

6. Where the Lord Jesus may have anticipated that he would locate the best confidence in himself, he found the most steady "unbelief." And despite the fact that he was the omniscient

Son of God, "he wondered" at his unbelieving associates. "He went." The Greek imperfect tense depicts the activity as in process. He was going from town to town, "educating" in each town. This service in Nazareth and in the towns is the principal phase of the third Galilean lecturing visit.

7. The second phase of the visit was presented when Jesus called The Twelve and "began" to "send them forward." This obviously was the first occasion when they had gone out without Christ, and it hence constituted a propelled venture in their preparation of "Power." Authority.

8. They were to "take nothing for their voyage." This was intended to prepare them in the act of confidence and readiness for when they would be alone. "No scrip." A voyaging sack for conveying arrangements. "Cash." This term alludes to little copper coins. They were not to take little change. "Purse." A belt or support was worn to hold the free Oriental pieces of clothing set up; it was additionally used to convey cash.

9. The goal was that they ought to take no additional wearing clothing. "Costs." The article of clothing alluded to is the underwear worn alongside the skin, instead of a coat.

11. They were to "shake off the dust" not in individual enmity but rather as a "testimony" to demonstrate the earnestness of dismissing the message of the Son of God. The announcement concerning "Sodom and Gomorrha" was not in the most punctual Greek compositions.

13. Blessing "with oil" was a typical restorative practice (cf. Lk. 10:34; Jas. 5:14)(Hobart, 2004) records various references from antiquated journalists to this impact. The ceremonial blessing of the debilitated did not show up until the second century (Swete,1953). In this manner, these healings were a mix of marvel and prescription.

14. The occurrence recorded in 6:14-29 happened amid the third voyage through Galilee (cf. vv.12,13,30). This "ruler Herod" was Herod Antipas, child of Herod the Great and tetrarch of Galilee and Perea. The proceeding with the service of Christ and his

followers in Galilee had spread his acclaim to all aspects of the district. Surprisingly, we have confirmed that the notoriety of Christ has been considered by government authorities.

15. A typical talk among the general population was that he was Elijah returning in satisfaction of Mal. 4:5 (cf. Matt. 16:14; Jn. 1:21), or that he was a "prophet" after the example of the OT prophets.

17. The "prison" where John was incarcerated was situated at Machaerus, on the eastern shore of the Dead Sea. The conjugal relationship of the Herods were shocking. Herodias was the wife of her half-uncle, Herod Philip I, yet she cleared him out to wed another half-uncle, his brother, Herod Antipas. Herod Antipas was already married to the daughter of Aretas, lord of Arabia; however, he set this spouse (wife) away.

18. "John had said." He was saying it over and over (repeatedly).

19. "Herodias had a quarrel against him. Truly, Mark says that she ceaselessly had it in for him. She, not at all like Herod, felt no appreciation

for John and his proclaiming; despite what might be expected, she continued needing to execute him.

20. With Herod it was distinctive. Regardless of his free-living, he was moved by John's life and message. "Watched him." Better, he secured him and would not enable Herodias to execute (kill) him. "He did many things." The most credible perusing says..... he was astounded. The contention between his appreciation for John and the fascination of his corrupt connections kept him in a condition of internal perplexity. In any case, he "listened (Gr. continued hearing) him readily."

21. Herodias had sat tight, trying to make it a "convenient day" to infiltrate Herod's protection of John. The tip top of the administrative, military, and groups of friends were welcomed ("rulers, commanders, boss domains," separately).

22. "The daughter" alluded to was Salome, the offspring of Herodias by past marriage. It is assessed that the young lady was close to twenty years of age right now (Taylor, 1953). For the little girl of a ruler to engage respectability in

this design was completely the strange. It was the work of a slave, not a princess. This, notwithstanding, was Herodias' lucky minute (v. 21), and Herod, under the influence of alcohol and arousing quality, fell into her trap. "Sat with him." Rather, leaned back with him (see 2:15).

25. The ask for of Herodias was set apart by criticalness. She needed the deed finished before Herod could figure out how to maintain a strategic distance from it. Salome returned "straightway with haste" and asked that her demand be in all actuality, not "by and by" (AV), but rather without a moment's delay (Gr.). "Charger." An antiquated word for a platter.

26. In spite of the fact that the demand profoundly lamented Herod, he thought that it was difficult to backpedal on his vows before such an august gathering. It was more vital to hide any hint of failure face than to safeguard the life of God's prophet. It was no big surprise that a while later, his still, small voice pained him (vv. 14,16).

27. Herod's castle at Machaerus was likewise a stronghold and, in that capacity, would have contained a "prison." Thus, the execution scene was not far away from the dining room.

28. It creates the impression that Salome stayed in the eating lobby until John was executed, and they "brought his head to her." The obvious serenity with which she made the demand and, after that, conveyed the shocking dish "to her mother" is characteristic of the calloused way of the young lady.

30. Having finished the incidental clarification concerning the destiny of John, Mark comes back to the disciples and the preaching tour. He doesn't record anything concerning the time devoured or the occasions that happened. He just reports that the apostles returned together once more.

The assignment, "apostle," is most proper here. The word talks about one sent forward on a mission, and the followers were coming back from such an assignment.

Christ's Withdrawals From Galilee
(6:31-9:50)

The Lord had so altogether secured Galilee with his message that Galileans knew about his service in each stroll of life. Among a large number of average folks, his prevalence remained at such a crest that they were prepared to set him up with a constraint as their ruler.

The hatred of the Jewish religious pioneers was perilously close to the breaking point. What's more, Herod himself had now progressed toward becoming practiced concerning the prevalence of Christ. The circumstance was taking care of business toward an untimely emergency, while up 'til now, the service of Christ had not been finished. The outcome was that Jesus made four precise withdrawals from Galilee, one toward the eastern shore of the ocean (6:31-56), one to the locale of Tyre and Sidon (7:24-30), one to Decapolis (7:31-8:9), and the fourth to Caesarea Philippi (8:10-9:50).

Amid this time, Christ was involved with the preparation of the twelve teachers in arrangement for the season of his death.

Withdrawal To The Eastern Shore Of The Lake *(6:31-56)*

This segment of the Gospel records the sustaining of the five thousand (6:31-44), the wonder of strolling on the water (6:45-52), and the healings on the plain of Gennesaret (6:53-56). Rather than being a time of rest and retirement from the group, it was a period of proceeding with movement.

31. The "forsake place" was presumably on the upper east shore of the Sea of Galilee. It was not forsaken; the expression signifies "an abandoned place, a wild." After the anxiety of the proclaiming visit, they expected to "rest a while."

33. "Many knew him." As individuals saw them leaving, they remembered that the group could expect where Christ was making a beeline to go before he appeared to affirm the

view that the wild place (v.31) was on the upper east shore of the lake.

34. At the point when Jesus landed (AV, "turned out"), it wound up plainly obvious that he and his men would not have the capacity to appreciate the arranged time of rest. In any case, his response was not one of inconvenience; rather, he was "moved with sympathy." He saw the general population in their need as shepherdless "sheep," having no otherworldly pioneer (cf. Num. 27:17; I Kgs. 22:17).

36. "Nation." Mark's pledge truly implies fields, which most likely alludes to the ranches of the wide open.

37. "Give ye." The accentuation is regarding the matter of "ye." The money-related term utilized here, "pennyworth," is the word denarion, the Roman denarius worth around eighteen pennies around then.

40. "In positions." The Greek expression implied a garden bed. Check's photo of the scene is that of gatherings of individuals scattered like beds of blooms on the green grass

(v. 39). Most likely, the variegated shades of the garments served to make such an impression when seen at a separation.

41. The verbs "had taken," "looked," "favored," and "brake" are all in the aorist tense in Greek, meaning momentary activity. In any case, the verb "gave" is in the blemished tense, appearing, interestingly, that he continued providing for the followers. It is now that the supernatural occurrence of an increased supply happened.

43. The astounding truth was not that the general population was just filled but rather that there was a superabundant supply. The "wicker bins" were expansive handbaskets utilized for conveying nourishment. All in all, be that as it may, they were smaller than the ones utilized at the bolstering of the four thousand (see remarks on 8:8).

44. The count of "five thousand" did exclude ladies and kids (cf. Matt. 14:21).

45. Christ " constrained his disciples," which states that he constrained them to enter the boat (not ship) and set sail "unto Bethsaida."

Evidently, the place of the supernatural occurrence was south of Bethsaida Julias (Lk. 9:10), and Christ guided the supporters to sail to the town and meet him there. The purpose behind this sudden scattering of the "general population," as given by John (6:14,15), was the risk of a progressive endeavor to make Jesus a king.

47. "When even was come." That is, when six o'clock, the hour of dusk, had arrived.

48. Since it was not yet dark, he could at present, observe them from the land "worked in paddling." "Toiling," from a verb intending to torment or trouble, pictures the trouble of the supporters as they endeavored to push into the opposite wind. The "fourth watch of the night" kept going from three to six in the morning.

Jesus deferred his going to their guide from dusk until around 3:00 A.M. The announcement that he "would have gone by them" ought not represent any issue concerning Christ's earnestness. He was not strolling specifically toward the boat, so to the disciples, it created the impression that he would have gone by on the off chance that they had not shouted out (v.49). Instead of abruptly entering the boat, Jesus was, most likely, giving them an opportunity to see him.

49. "A spirit." This is not the Greek word for "spirit" but rather a term that implies an apparition. They thought they were seeing a ghost.

50. "Be of good cheer." This verb conveys with it the possibility of boldness and courage, which was presumably the idea highest in the mind of Christ. The current state of disallowance, "be not afraid," means quit fearing.

51. Without a word from Christ, "the wind stopped" (Gr. Becoming weary), and it's blowing. The bewilderment that was grasping the disciples was the aftereffect of a twofold supernatural occurrence. The Greek content precludes the words "and wondered."

52. Not only had they overlooked that Christ had already stilled the waves (4:39), but they didn't comprehend (Gr. content) the marvel "of the loaves." Because "their hearts were

hardened," they didn't get a handle on the truth concerning the deity of Christ, which the supernatural occurrences were persistently illustrating.

53. Jesus presumably entered the boat someplace off the shore from Bethsaida Julias, after which they "passed over" toward the western shore of the lake once more. "Gennesaret" was the name of the plain lying along the shore of the lake south of Capernaum. A residential area of a similar name was additionally situated in the region.

55. Marks gives a look at the sort of scene that, more likely than not, seemed common when Jesus went to a region. The general population rushed to bring their sick folk before Christ moved from their neighborhood.

56. "Besought him." The rehashed solicitations of a great many persons are portrayed by this verb. This is the second reference in Mark to healings affected by touching Christ's garment (cf. 5:27-29).

Chapter Seven

Discussion Of The Unwarranted Exaltation Of Tradition (7:1-23)

These verses record the conflict amongst Christ and the Pharisees on the essential issue of the wellspring of authority. Does custom tradition convey divine expertise? Is it equivalent to, or predominant to, the composed Word of God? Likewise, the talk of the genuine way of defilement and cleansing is included here. The setting for the area clearly was the region of Capernaum.

Mark's clarification of Jewish traditions is vital, showing as it does that this Gospel was composed for Gentile utilization. "Defiled..... hands." Hands formally unclean. "They found fault" does not show up in the best manuscripts. The sentence is left inadequate as Mark severs to present the clarification of verses 3,4.

3. "The Pharisees" had so augmented their impact that the washing of the hands had, for the most part, turned into the act of "a considerable number of Jews." The Greek text does not bolster the utilization of "oft."

Instead, it peruses with a clenched hand (a fist), presumably alluding to the demonstration of rubbing the clenched hand of one submit the palm of the other when washing.

The corpus of the summons and lessons of the respected rabbis of the previous, a group of 613 principles intended to direct every part of life.

6. Jesus did not imply that Isaiah particularly anticipated the acts of the principal century Jews, but rather that Isaiah's words concerning the general population of his own day were material in addition to the Jews of Christ's day. The citation is from Isaiah 29:13, after the LXX, with slight change. The expression "hypocrites" is a designation well picked, for it alluded initially to an on-screen character who wore a mask and seemed, by all accounts, to be what he truly was definitely not.

The fundamental purpose of the citation from Isaiah concerns the substitution of "the tradition of men for the decree (commandment) of God." This is not an exaggeration, for the Pharisees saw oral custom as being more definitive than the composed law of the OT.

10. In 7:9-13 this praise of custom is given particular delineation. The law of "Moses" concerning honor to parents is cited. The primary reference is from Deut. 5:16 and is indistinguishable from both the Hebrew and the LXX. The second, which is from Exod. 21:17 takes after the Hebrew content nearly.

11. Interestingly, Christ refers to the rabbinical tradition that puts aside the God-given Mosaic commandment. "Corban" is the transliteration of a Hebrew word meaning a gift, as Mark clarifies for the advantage of his Gentile readers. The word was utilized to allude to something given to God by a promise which was inviolable. In the event that a son announced that the sum expected to bolster his parents was "Corban," that promise was unalterable, notwithstanding putting aside the Mosaic command.

13. The "word of God" is put in sharp complexity to the tradition of men. Notice that Christ saw the Mosaic law as having been spoken by God. To make "of no effect" is to make void or to invalidate, to nullify. The

current state, "do ye," talks about frequent practice.

14. In verses 14-16, the ruler comes back to the subject of pollution and purifying; however, here he is talking to the Pharisees and copyists as well as to the group whom "he had called" together. In this way, Christ talks about the matter with his disciples (7:17-23).

15. "Nothing from without a man" - that is, nothing physical - can defile him ethically or profoundly, morally or spiritually. For the situation under discussion (v.2), eating with unwashed hands can't deliver otherworldly uncleanness (spiritual uncleanness). Such defilement is interior in inception. A man is contaminated by considerations that begin in the heart and turn out in the types of words or actions.

In this, Jesus clarified the spiritual essentialness of the laws of the clean and unclean (Lev. 11). One reason why they were offered was to show this very truth of spiritual defilement. However, these Jewish leaders never got past the negligible facades (mere externals).

19. The "heart" in Biblical utilization is not only the seat of feelings but also the place of mental and volitional movement. It alludes to the internal, nonphysical man. "The belly" alludes to the body cavity that contains the stomach and digestive organs. After the stomach-related process is finished, the rest is "out into the draught," that is, into the deplete (drain). The AV does not clarify what is implied by the expression "purging all meats."

The best clarification is that it ought to be associated with "he saith" (v.18). Jesus, by his explanation in 7:18,19, declared all food to be "clean." he put aside the Levitical refinement between the clean and unclean (cf. Acts 10:14, 15).

20-22. These verses contain Jesus' explanation of what he implied by "that which cometh out of the man." The "evil thoughts" (underhanded musings) are to be comprehended as being evil reasoning, detestable explanations or outlines, and think considerations. The word for "deceit" conveys the more intense meaning of foul play, the connotation of treachery.

"Lasciviousness" is uncontrolled and unconcealed unethical behavior. The words "evil eye" in whatever other culture than that of the Jews could allude to the throwing of a spell. Among the Jews, be that as it may, it is an expression of envy. In this setting, "foolishness" is more moral than intellectual.

Withdrawal To The Region Of Tyre And Sidon *(7:24-30)*

In this concise segment, Mark reports a fairly extensive voyage of Christ to the locale of Phoenicia, where the occurrence with the Syrophoenician woman happened.

24. "The Borders of Tire and Sidon." An informal expression for the area of Tyre and Sidon. This was the main time, so far as the record goes, when Christ left Palestine into the entirely Gentile domain. His motivation for these visits outside Galilee was not fundamentally to minister to the multitudes but rather to teach (instruct) his disciples, which is the motivation behind why he "would have no man know" that he was there.

26. "A Greek." This is the same as recognizing the woman as a Gentile. By birth, she was a Syrian from the Phoenician region. "She besought him." Mark's utilization of the Greek imperfect tense pictures the request demand of the woman. "Devil." It should be deciphered as "evil spirit, demon."

27. Jesus utilized the expression "children" to speak to represent the Jews. His central mission was first to the Jews all together that they may, thusly, satisfy their obligation of turning into a gift, a blessing to all countries through the overall announcement of the Gospel.

"The dogs." This was a typical Jewish term rebuke connected to Gentiles. Nonetheless, it is relaxed by the utilization of the humble frame signifying "little dogs" or "puppies." These were the family pets, not the wild canines of the road.

28. The woman's unafraid answer was the reaction of faith. "The dogs under the table." Taking up Christ's minor term for dogs, she paints a touching scene of the puppies licking up the scraps dropped by the children. All she

solicited was a piece (a crumb) from the blessings accessible to the Jews.

29. Jesus perceived in "this saying" of the woman the proof of bona fide faith (cf. Matt. 15:28). As of now, as He talked, the evil spirit had left (Gr. perfect tense) her little girl. The one-of-a-kind component of this supernatural occurrence was that it was performed at a separation with no vocal order from Christ.

Withdrawal To Decapolis (7:31-8:9)

The arrival from the locale of Tyre and Sidon did not take Christ back to Galilee; rather, his course evaded the eastern shore of the lake, driving him into the Decapolis. There, Jesus mended the hard of hearing man who had an impediment of speech (7:31-37), and he fed the crowd of 4,000.

31. Mark is the most unequivocal of the Gospel authors now. He discloses to us that Jesus left the locale of "Tyre" and went through "Sidon" roughly twenty-five miles toward the north, diving deep into the Gentile domain. At that

point, turning south, he go along the eastern shore of the Sea of Galilee into the locale of Decapolis (see 5:20).

32. The degree of the "impediment of speech" is begging to be proven wrong. Mogilalon might be utilized by one who is totally quiet, yet its strict significance is that talking with trouble appears to demonstrate that, beforehand, he had not possessed the capacity to talk. In any case, the shout of the general population at 7:37 was that he made them speechless to talk.

33. That it was a bit much for the Lord to touch a man with a specific end goal to heal him had been exhibited already (cf. 2:3-12; 3:5; 7:29,30). Here, Jesus "put his fingers" into the deaf man's ears to demonstrate what he would accomplish for him and, in this manner, to help him to believe.

Two other symbolic acts were taken after. "He spits" and "He touched his tongue." The content does not state that He connected the salivation to the tongue.

34. "He sighed." The word may allude to a groan. Maybe this was an outflow of sensitivity or of trouble as a result of distress or the misery of mankind.

"Ephphatha." An Aramaic word that Mark deciphers for his Gentile perusers.

35. "The string of his tongue." The bond that held his tongue was discharged. "Plain." He started to talk properly or doubtlessly (more exceedingly).

36. Christ still expected to maintain a strategic distance from unreasonable exposure (cf. on 5:43). In any case, the general population would not be stilled. They continued declaring the supernatural occurrence more exceedingly.

37. "Beyond measure." The wonder (astonishment) of the general population surpassed all limits. Mark utilizes an exceptionally solid word here (hyperperissos).

Chapter Eight

The Feeding Of The Four Thousand
(8:1-9)

The feeding of the four thousand is not given a particular setting other than the general proclamation that it happened in a wild place (v.4).

1. "In those days." The Greek content includes "again," likely with reference to the current sustaining of the five thousand.

2. Jesus was moved with "compassion" at the general population, similarly as he had been on the event of the feeding of the five thousand (6:34); however, here, his concern was brought about by their physical need instead of by their otherworldly condition.

6. Here, as in the feeding of the five thousand, the words "took," "gave thanks," and "brake" are all in the aorist tense in Greek, yet "gave" is in the imperfect tense, demonstrating that Christ continued giving the bread to the disciples for distribution (cf. 6:41).

8. The adequacy of the marvel is found in the statements that they "were filled" and that there

was an abundance that "was left." The word "meat," embedded by the interpreters of the AV, alludes to food when all is said and done. These "baskets" were of an alternate sort than those utilized after the encouragement of the five thousand.

This is demonstrated by the refinement made between the two sorts in 8:19,20 (Gr. content). The sort of basket utilized this time was regularly very substantial.

It was the kind used to let Saul down over the wall at Damascus (Acts 9:25). In this manner, the seven hampers of 8:8 most likely held more than the twelve provision baskets of 6:43.

Withdrawal To Caesarea Philippi
(8:10-9:50)

The fourth and last withdrawal from Galilee was northward into the district of Caesarea Philippi. Originating from Decapolis, Jesus crossed toward the west shoreline of the Sea of Galilee, where the Pharisees met him with a demand for a sign (8:10-12). He then went by watercraft in a northeasterly heading to Bethsaida Julias (8:13-21), where he recuperated a visually impaired man (8:22-26).

From that point, his voyage took him overland to the region of Caesarea Philippi. Here once more, Christ's primary action was that of educating his pupils concerning such subjects as his individual, his demise and revival, their discipleship, and his coming in brilliance as prefigured by the Transfiguration (8:27-9:13).

Here, additionally, he cured another demoniac (9:14-29. After this, Christ comes back to Galilee, proceeding with the direction of the Twelve (9:30-50).

10. Right now, researchers can't pinpoint the town of "Dalmanutha" with any level of conviction. The setting appears to accept an area over the sea from Bethsaida, most likely on the western shore (cf. vv. 13,22). Matthew calls it Magadan (Matt. 15:39; Gr. content), a place similarly obscure to us today.

11. "The Pharisees" were requesting a staggering sign from God that would demonstrate that Jesus was the Messiah. "Tempting him." The Greek word peirazo signifies "to test." Rather than

endeavoring to allure Jesus to sin, they were putting him under a magnifying glass (testing him) of their unbelieving personalities.

12. Such steady refusal to accept (believe) made Christ sigh "deeply in his spirit." The word, showing up here in its heightened frame, most likely implies that he really moaned as the feeling of exhaustion and melancholy grief infiltrated the profundities of his heart.

The subject of Christ is better deciphered. Why is this era (this generation) consistently looking for a sign? (cf. Jn. 2:18; Matt. 12:38). Matthew adds an exemption to the statement of Christ that "no sign" would be given (Matt. 16:4).

The indication of Jonah is clarified in Matthew 12:39,40 as alluding to Christ's restoration, the most critical marvel of all.

15. Jesus "charged them" over and again, demonstrating that the dire should be ceaselessly protected ("take heed, be careful"). Leaven is here used to symbolize something with a perilously unavoidable impact. Luke 12:1 clarifies that "the leaven of the Pharisees" is deception (hypocrisy). The "leaven of Herod" might be the impact of the

Herodians, which was a soul of experience, an irresistible secularism.

19-20. The disciples had so soon overlooked the lessons natural to the feedings of the "five thousand" and the "four thousand." The Son of God does not have to stress over nourishment for thirteen men on a short voyage over the lake. He had yet, as of late, shown his power to supply nourishment for more than nine thousand people.

22. The mending of the "blind man" happened when Jesus has gone through "Bethsaida" Julias while in transit to Caesarea Philippi.

23. Jesus "led him out of the town," most likely to keep away from extreme public exposure (cf. v.26). Here, as on account of the hard of hearing man (7:33), salvia was utilized, not as a recuperating application, but rather as a guide to the blind man's faith.

24. This healing was special in that it comprised two phases. After the main healing acts, the man saw individuals indistinguishably as moving items, similar to "trees strolling."

25. The second phase of healing was going before the touching of the eyes. The Greek content does not state that Jesus "made him look up," but instead that the man looked eagerly. What's more, when he did as such, he saw all things "unmistakably, clearly."

26. Again, with a specific end goal to maintain a strategic distance from the aftereffects of undue exposure (publicity), Christ sent the man "to his home." That He let him know not to "go into the town" shows that he lived somewhere else, maybe in the encompassing wide open.

27. Going north from Bethsaida, Christ came "to the town of Caesarea Philippi." Matthew (16:13) clarifies that he came into the parts of the area of Caesarea.

Mark has reference to the towns situated in the nation encompassing the bigger city. This Caesarea, situated in the northwest area of the tetrarchy of Philip, was assigned Philippi to recognize it from Caesarea as the Mediterranean drift.

29. "Whom say ye." This was the time when Christ was pointing. The accentuation is on

"you." "However, you (as opposed to others), who do you say that I am?" "Peter" gone about as a representative for the disciples. His admission of Jesus as "the Christ" is completely given in Matt. 16:16, which includes the words "the Son of the living God." Jesus is both the guaranteed Messiah and the unique Son of God.

30. Here again, Christ instructed quiet, most likely on account of the progressive thoughts associated with the Messianic idea. Christ was not prepared around then to build up a natural Messianic kingdom.

31. Rather, at his initial coming, Christ was to "suffer," "be slaughtered (killed)," and "rise again." Particular consideration ought to be given to the sharp difference between the sparkling admission of Peter and Christ's quick revelation of suffering and death. Notice that the One who was to die was assigned by the Messianic title, "Son of man." The cross was an essential part of Messiah's work. "He must suffer."

32. "He spake.....openly." The Greek flawed tense is utilized to demonstrate that Jesus started and kept on discussing his demise. At no time in the future did he allude to it in hidden form (cf. Jn.

2:19), yet from this time on, he trained his disciples "straightforwardly" and expressly concerning the reality. This was the following stage in their preparation. "Peter approached him" and reprimanded him for talking in such a way. In Peter's mind, a violent death did not fit Messianic dignity.

33. Peter's endeavor to prevent the Lord from heading off to the cross was like the enticement in the wild. In this example, "Satan," with incredible subtility, utilized one of Christ's wardrobe followers (cf. Lk. 4:13. RSV). See the comparative censure in Matt. 4:10. "Savourest." The Greek verb alludes to the arrangement of the psyche, the bearing of thought. Peter's brain was running in opposition to the purposes of God.

34. The instruction recorded in 8:34-38 is the common outgrowth of the reality of Christ's suffering. "Whosoever will come after" Christ must walk the way which he walked, the way of disavowal denial) and cross-bearing.

The "cross" is simply the image of affliction and suffering and speaks of readiness to suffer for another person. Christ is the example; the disciple is to continue following him.

35. The Catch 22 of these verses is settled by understanding that the Lord utilized the expression "life" in two distinct faculties. The main expression, "save his life," is a reference to the protection of physical life from death. The individual who is totally committed to the assurance of this life will miss the life that is endless.

Unexpectedly, the individual who is so committed to Christ that he will "lose his life" is the individual who increases genuine life (eternal life). He finds that "to die is to gain" (Phil. 1:21). This is not a depiction of the method for salvation for the lost, but instead of the rationality of life for the disciple.

36. Here, the differentiation is amongst "world" and "soul." The last term is the same as "life" in verse 35. Both are interpretations of the mind. This guideline applies on the physical level and additionally on the spiritual level. What is the benefit of getting all the world brings to the table if a man bites the dust and can't appreciate it? What is the benefit of storing up a universe of natural belonging for a couple of short years on

the off chance that it implies the loss of eternal life?

38. At the point when Christ utilized the expression, "ashamed of me and of my words," he was drawing an appearance differently in relation to the mentality of readiness to lose one's life for his purpose and the Gospel's (v.35). To "be ashamed" is to deny Christ in the hour of trial as opposed to possess him even at the danger of death.

It is to stand firm with this "sinful generation" rather than with Christ. "Adulterous." Used profoundly (spiritually) to portray unfaithfulness to God. In like way, when the Lord comes as Judge, he will "be ashamed" and will disown the individuals who have abandoned disowned him.

Chapter Nine

Conclusion Of Discourse (9:1-50)

The section division here is appalling since this verse is obviously the conclusion of the talk recorded in the last portion of Mark 8. "Verily" is a term of serious affirmation (solemn assurance). It is the Greek word amen, from which our "amen" is inferred. "Shall not taste of death." The first is considerably more grounded - might in no way, shape, or form taste of death.

The happening to "the kingdom of God" in this statement has been differently deciphered (interpreted). Be that as it may, in the previous verse, Christ talks about his coming in glory (his advent in glory), and in the accompanying verses, Mark records the Transfiguration. The happening to the Kingdom may well be indistinguishable from the transcendent happening to the King (8:38), of which Christ's transfiguration was a preview.

2. The "high mountain" was generally recognized as Mount Tabor in Galilee, yet this is also a long way from Caesarea Philippi. Mount Hermon appears to fit the portrayal all the more palatably. "Transfigured." The Greek metamorphoo

(source of our metamorphosis") alludes to a change of fundamental shape, not a shallow change of outward appearance. One Lord's human body was glorified, and it is in this glorified body that he will someday come to set up his kingdom.

3. "As snow." Not found in the best Greek compositions. A "more full" is one who treats new fabric, contracting and purging it.

4. "Elias" is the transliteration of the Greek word for Elijah. Why Moses and Elijah were the two showed up is not expressed. It is essential that both left this life under abnormal conditions. Besides, Moses spoke to the Law, while Elijah was one of the prophets. Luke's Gospel (9:31) states that the subject of their discussion was the inescapable death of Christ, a topic which goes through the OT, both in the Law and in the Prophets.

6. "Wist." The old English word for "knew." "Sore anxious." They were panicked, terrified.

9. The charge "that they ought to tell no man" was with regards to Jesus' arrangement of restriction, keeping in mind that the current

incorrect Messianic thoughts be fanned into blazes.

After the Resurrection, the peril of encouraging a famous uprising would never again be available. At that point, the experience on the mount would have a profound incentive (spiritual value) for the disciples as an affirmation of their faith (cf. II Pet. 1:16-18).

11. The question concerning Elijah emerged due to the nearness of the prophet at Transfiguration. "The scribes," in this example, drew their instructing from Mal. 4:5,6. It might have been that the disciples were thinking about whether the appearance on the mount was the fulfillment of the prediction.

12. This prophecy received affirmation by the Lord, and the strain utilized (futuristic present) shows that it should be satisfied later on (in the future). Elijah will come and reestablish all things (cf. Mal. 4:6) preceding the Messiah comes. "How it is written." Most understudies view the rest of this verse as a question, "How is it written.....?" The happening to Elijah was anticipated in the Scriptures.

Shouldn't something be said about the forecasts that the Messiah ought to endure and be rejected? Christ endeavored to mix the reasoning of his disciples so that they may comprehend that the Son of man should first suffer and be rejected before the happening to Elijah and the transcendent appearance of Messiah.

13. Be that as it may, there was a sense in which Elijah had as of now come. Matthew 17:13 clarifies that He was talking about John the Baptist. This was not to state that John was Elijah face to face, yet that he came in the similarity of Elijah (cf. Lk. 1:17; Jn. 1:21). "At all they recorded." That is, they did with him what they sought, alluding to his demise at the demand of Herodias.

15. "Greatly amazed." The clarifications of this wonder can all be decreased to two potential outcomes. One, they were astonished as a result of the rest of the shine of the Transfiguration all over. Two, the wonder was created by the advantageous yet unforeseen appearance of Jesus right now of the humiliating thrashing of the nine pupils. The primary view is rendered doubtful by

the nonappearance of any announcement concerning a proceeding with sparkle all over.

17. The "dumb spirit" was a demon that tormented the boy with dullness and deafness (v. 25).

18. "Taketh him." The father depicted the demon's activity of seizing or laying hold on the boy. His response seems to have been like that of an epileptic fit.

19. unmistakably, the disciples were frail in light of unbelief. The mistake of our Lord appears to be practically to skirt on impatience. Suffer. Truly, How long might I endure you (how long shall I put up with you)?

20. "Tare." This is a solid word implying that he shook the boy with such brutality that it appeared he would tear him into pieces. "Wallowed." The Greek word intends to roll. The flawed tense ought to be deciphered; He continued rolling.

23. "If thou canst." In the Greek content, an article goes before this entire condition with the end goal of attracting consideration regarding it. It is as if Jesus stated, "Consider this provision -

"if thou canst." "Believe" does not show up in the best manuscripts. Having pointed out the man's "if," Jesus continued to demonstrate his need for faith.

24. The anguish that filled the father's heart is depicted by this quick reaction as he "cried out" in practically opposing discharges. He did "believe," but then he was intensely aware of the "unbelief" that battled with his craving to trust verifiably. His unbelief was not an adamant refusal to trust; it was a shortcoming with which the man himself couldn't bargain. Consequently, his cry to Christ for assistance.

29. "This kind." A sign that there are distinctive sorts of evil spirits. It appears that the one indwelling this boy was abnormally awful and effective. From Jesus' past comment about unbelief (v.19) and from the statement in this verse concerning the need for "prayer," it is evident that the nine disciples had endeavored to cast out the evil spirit without depending upon God's power (cf. Matt. 17:20).

Unbelief and prayerlessness are certain to bring about spiritual impotency. A large number of the best Greek original copies exclude the reference to "fasting" and the parallel entry in Matt. 17:21. It is to be noticed that there would have been no open door for the disciples to meet this circumstance with fasting; however, they, without a doubt, could have trusted and prayed.

31. "He taught his disciples." This had been the Lord's primary occupation amid the withdrawals, and still, he kept training them, for they were eased back (slow) to comprehend (v. 32). The heart of his instructing was his coming death and resurrection.

33. The arrival "to Capernaum" conveyed him again to the "house" of Peter, which had been the home office for his Galilean crusade.

The verb "asked" is in the imperfect tense, most likely to demonstrate that Jesus kept on scrutinizing the disciples concerning their discussion on the road.

34. rather than answering Jesus' cross-examination, "they held their peace." Again, the imperfect tense demonstrates that they persisted in their silence. They were embarrassed to uncover the unworthy subject of their talk. He had attempted to clarify his coming death, yet

their psyches were possessed with considerations of individual significance (personal greatness) in the Messianic kingdom (see Matt. 18:1).

36-37. The unassuming demonstration of accepting one "child" in Christ's name is a deed of genuine enormity. It is this readiness to take the humble position of administration, even to a child in arms, which is the characteristic of bona fide stature, for to do as such is to render service to Christ and, through him, to the Father. This includes the lowering of one's self as a little child (Matt. 18:4).

38. Maybe a longing to change the subject drove "John" to talk. Obviously, Jesus' comment concerning acts done in his name helped John remember the exorcists whom they had seen and who utilized the name of Jesus. "Master." This is the word for "teacher." "We forbad him." They continued restricting this obscure wonder laborer (unknown miracle worker). Their reason, "he followeth not us," uncovers an essentially egotistical state of mind, an unwillingness to acknowledge anybody aside from those of their own circle. Scofield calls this sectarianism.

39. "Deny him not." Literally, Stop precluding him. Jesus did not bandy about points of interest. On the off chance that the man was utilizing Christ's name in an earnest push to help other people, he was not to be ruined. An expansiveness of the soul that should describe God's people is confirmed here. Our Lord's rationale was two-collapsed. To begin with, such a man would not soon betray Christ in the wake of working wonders in His name.

40. The second explanation behind Christ's restriction was that since the man was not "against" Christ and the disciples, then to some degree, he was on their side.

41. This verse additionally underlines the expansiveness of disposition shown in 9:39,40. Nobody who is trying to serve the Lord, regardless of how apparently immaterial his service might be, is prohibited from Christ's circle. The significance of this guideline is found in the utilization of "verily" (so be it) and in the solid twofold negative, which might be translated as "will in no way, shape or form lose his reward."

42. The prospect of this verse is connected to that of 9:37 by the expression "little ones." Likewise,

verses 42-48 are connected, being based on the possibility of offenses.

It is conceivable that the activity of the disciples in reprimanding the mysterious exorcist (v.38) may have insulted him. This would clarify why Christ talked about offenses now. The undeveloped faith of the exorcist was not to be thwarted but rather empowered.

Unforgiving feedback of profound adolescence (spiritual immaturity) may just serve to push people far from the Lord. "Offend." The Greek word skandalizo intends to put a catch or trap in a man's way, making him lurch. The "little ones" might be taken truly as alluding to children who believe, or they might be the individuals who are little in faith or profoundly undeveloped spiritually. Presumably, the last is Jesus's expectation. The "millstone" was the vast level stone turned by a jackass in pounding grain.

43. Jesus turned from the offense of others to the offense of one's self. It is workable for a man to put a hindrance in his own particular manner. Without a doubt, the summon to "cut .... off" the culpable "hand" is metaphorical and hyperbolic. The feeling of the verse is that anything that

makes a man fall into transgression (sin) ought to be removed quickly.

These verses are not to be taken truly as instructing an outrageous self-denial. It must be recalled that the seat of wrongdoing is the spirit, no organ of the physical body. "Go into life." The parallel expression in 9:47 is "go into the kingdom of God."

These terms are the alternate extremes of "hell" and are to be comprehended as alluding to the life of the spared in the everlasting kingdom. "hell " is the interpretation of the Greek geena, which thusly is a transliteration of the Hebrew ge Hinnom, signifying "valley of Hinnom." This was a valley southwest of Jerusalem which was damned since it had been the scene of Moloch's love.

Later, it turned into the site of the city dump, where consistent flames were consumed, decreasing the trash to fiery debris. The waste and decline saved there would likewise have been swarmed with many worms. In Jewish thought, this valley turned into the image of the place of everlasting discipline.

48. The dialect of this verse is taken from the LXX of Isa. 66:24. The worm that "dieth not" is a more interesting method of expression drawn from the real valley of Hinnom, where worms were consistently at work. It is a photo of the unending torment and annihilation of hellfire.

49. The verse and the accompanying are among the most troublesome in the Gospels. To start with, it ought to be noted that the second provision of 9:49 was most likely a later expansion since it has poor original copy bolster. It might have been a minimal endeavor to clarify this troublesome section.

The initial word "for" (gar) would regularly attach this statement to the previous one, in which case it serves to support or clarify the previous declaration (assertion). It might then imply that everybody who enters damnation should be protected as salt preserves through an unfathomable length of time (an eternity) of torment.

50. Taking up "salt," utilized as a part of 9:49 regarding hell, Jesus goes ahead to state that Christ's followers are to be as salt, giving their impact a chance to be felt on the planet (cf. Matt.

5:13). "Have salt in yourselves." He instructed the disciples to be penetrated with this cleaning impact.

Keeping in mind the end goal of having a healthy impact, they should themselves be the holders of this healthiness. "Have tranquility." Christ finishes up with one last reference to the disagreement regarding enormity recorded in 9:343. Both charges are in their current state, requiring a persevering, enduring practice.

Chapter Ten

Christ's Ministry In Perea (10:1-52)

With one explanation, Mark compresses around six months of Christ's service (v.1). His say of Judea covers the later Judean period, which is recorded to a great extent in Jn. 7:10-10:39 and Lk. 10:1-13:21; the reference to "the more remote side of Jordan" needs to do with the Perean service, most of which is accounted for by Mk. 10:2-52 are, as a general rule, the end occasions of this Perean period (cf. Lk. 18:15-19:28).

Discussions Of Divorce, Children, And Wealth (10:1-31)

These discussions presumably happened someplace in Perea. No correct area is given. In 10:2-12, Christ addressed the Pharisees' cross-examination concerning the legitimateness of separation (divorce); 10:13-16 shows Jesus' disposition toward youngsters; and 10:17-31 records the happening to the rich youthful ruler and the resultant talk of riches.

1. "From thence." Jesus left Capernaum, where he had stopped briefly at Peter's home (9:33). "Coasts" is better interpreted as regions. There is a vital printed issue here concerning the expression "Judaea by the farther side of Jordan." The original copy proves to favor the perusing Judea and the more distant side of Jordan.

At first, this seems, by all accounts, to be outlandish content since it appears to have switched Perea and Judea's normal requests. Originating from Galilee, Jesus would have experienced Perea, to begin with, and afterward through Judea. Be that as it may, this trouble is expelled by review 10:1 as a synopsis of the later Judean and the Perean times of Christ's service.

Taking after the time of withdrawals, Jesus went first to Judea for three months; then, he went to Perea for roughly a similar period of time. Therefore, the request in Mark's synopsis - Judea first and after that Perea - is right. "As he was wont." That is, just like his custom. The verb "educated" implies a proceeding with an event. For cases of this education, see entries such as Lk. 13:22-18:14.

2. The question posed by "the Pharisees" concerned one of the subjects that was talked about that day. The scribes who followed after Hillel held that a man could separate his better half for any cause. The supporters of Shammai, then again, demanded that separation be legal just in the event of infidelity. "Tempting." is a similar Greek word that may mean either "to entice, to tempt" or "to test."

Their question was put with an ulterior intention, keeping in mind the end goal to test Christ.

4. "Suffered." That is, Moses allowed separation (divorce). The Mosaic regulation is found in Deut. 24:1. It is to be noticed that the Pharisees did not express the condition under which Moses allowed separation.

5. "For the hardness of your heart." The stipulation of Moses was not a general rule or command but rather a concession on account of man's inadmissible profound condition. It was an endeavor to manage and control divorce instead of to encourage it.

6-8. The statement starting "God made them" (v.6) and finishing "shall be one flesh" (v.8) is taken verbatim from Gen. 1:27; 2:24 (LXX). The condition which existed in "the beginning " is demonstrative of God's ideal. He implied marriage to be a deep-rooted union in all cases.

11. The man, in this situation, confers "adultery against her," not in view of the divorce but rather in view of remarriage. In spite of the fact that he has experienced the legitimate separation method (legal divorce procedure) in God's sight, he is as yet hitched to his first spouse. Matthew includes the exception of fornication (Matt. 19:9).

13. The occasions recorded in this verse most likely occurred in the house (cf. v.10). "Brought." They continued bringing (Greek content) the children. The disposition of the disciples appears to have been founded on the origination that the Lord's opportunity was too profitable to possibly be squandered on children.

14. The interpretation of "abundantly disappointed, or much displeased" is not sufficiently commanding to speak to the Greek

verb, which intends to be rankled. Mark's Gospel is special in its portrayal of the feelings of Christ. "Suffer." Used in the feeling of "allow." Jesus' restriction actually implies Stopping or prohibiting them (or forbidding them).

The reason he offers for his activity is that the kingdom of God is comprised of such people. Unmistakably, he had the present spiritual kingdom as a primary concern.

16. The age of these children is proposed by the way that Jesus "took them up in his arms." He "blessed them" is a compound verb portraying the genuine enthusiasm with which Christ uttered the words of blessing (cf. Gen. 14:19-20; 27:26-29; 48:15-20).

17. The discussion with the rich, youthful ruler occurred as Jesus was going out where he had held up, most likely someplace in Perea (cf. v.10). Mark just expresses that "there came one running," however he doesn't say that the man was a youthful synagogue ruler. These realities are given by Matthew and Luke. "Master." This is the word for "teacher" (didaskale). He

thought about "eternal life" as something to be earned by doing good (Matt. 19:16).

18. The question. "Why callest thou me good?" was gone for driving the young fellow to consider the genuine personality, the true identity of Jesus. It was a circuitous declaration of His divinity since goodness or sinlessness is the nature of God alone.

19. Christ referred to some of "the commandments" without respect for their request in Exod. 20. The charge, "Defraud not," might be planned to speak to the tenth commandment, which concerns covetousness. The motivation behind pointing out the Law was to demonstrate to the young fellow his powerlessness to increase eternal life by acts of kindness (good works).

20. "All these have I observed." The young fellow could honestly make such a claim, yet his honesty was an external obedience. It was as the nobility or righteousness of the scribes and Pharisees (Matt. 5:20; cf. Phil. 3:6).

21. "Beholding him." Jesus looked eagerly and searchingly at him, and "He loved him." No

uncertainty He perceived the genuineness of the man's scan for something to meet his otherworldly need; He saw the potential spoken to in this upright, youthful pioneer.

22. At that point, He went to the heart of the man's issue, his commitment to his riches as opposed to God. In that lay the "one thing" he lacked. Keeping in mind the end goal to "follow after" Jesus, he should evacuate the snag of his affection for cash. It was not works of philanthropy that would pick up for him eternal life; it was getting to be noticeably related (identified with) to Christ.

23. The Lord did not deny the likelihood that a rich individual can be saved. He only said that it is troublesome.

"The kingdom of God" is the present, spiritual kingdom made out of the regenerated people of God (Jn. 3:3,5).

25. The possibility that "the eye of a needle," alluded to here, was a little door through which a camel could enter just on his knees without warrant. The word for "needle" alludes particularly to a sewing needle. Moreover, Jesus

was not discussing what man considers conceivable but rather about what is by all accounts inconceivable (cf. v.27). With man, it is unimaginable for "a camel to go through the eye" of a sewing needle.

29-30. "Verily" presents an announcement of grave confirmation. "Wife" is excluded in the better Greek writings. "A hundredfold." The things specified here might be taken actually to allude to such things as the many homes that will be opened to God's workers and the numerous new connections in the family unit of God.

On the other hand, they might be taken as metaphorically depicting the complex otherworldly gifts that the Lord piles upon the individuals who tail him conciliatorily. The "world to come," in the first dialect, is the coming age. It references the everlasting state to be introduced by Messiah's second appearance and the occasions associated with it, for example, the Day of the Lord, destructive judgments, the Millennium, and the final assize.

Conversation On The Way To Jerusalem
(10:32-45)

The discussion recorded in these verses occurred someplace in Perea as Jesus was en route, for the last time, to Jerusalem. Again, he rehashed the attestations concerning his death and resurrection (vv. 32-34), endeavoring by redundancy to put forth the realities for his disciples. What's more, again, the allurement to look for self-progression tormented the disciples (vv. 35-45).

32. This voyage "to Jerusalem" was, as Jesus knew, the one that would take him to his death. The way that "Jesus went before them," walking alone, was an astounding departure from his standard routine with regard to friendship (companionship) with his disciples. Probably, there was something about his weird standoffish quality that "amazed" them and made them "afraid." The tenses utilized here show this was a proceeding with a circumstance that continued for quite a while.

33-34. Progress past predictions is obvious in the quantity of points of interest given (cf.

8:31; 9:31). See the announcement, "We go up to Jerusalem," which shows that the satisfaction of those predictions would come amid this visit to the city.

However, the disciples still did not comprehend what Christ was endeavoring to disclose to them (Lk. 18:34). Their idea of the Messiah drove them to think just as far as glory and kingship (cf. Mk. 10:35-37).

35. Matthew expresses that "James" and "John" accompanied their mother and made their demand through her (20:20). Matthew likewise says, "Then came,".... which may show that this selfish demand of the two disciples took after quickly on the Savior's teaching concerning his death.

37. The "right hand" of a lord was the place of respect (honor), and the "left hand" was next in significance. "In thy glory." Or "in thy kingdom" (Matt. 20:21), which clarifies that the disciples had the glory of the Messianic kingdom at the top of the priority list.

38. The Lord, perceiving that they asked in ignorance, started to demonstrate to them that

such rewards must be earned. "The Cup" and "The Baptism" discuss Christ's agony, into which the disciple must be capable and willing to enter. In Gethsemane, he talks about his death as a "cup" (14:36); in Lk. 12:50, the expression "baptism" is a figure for suffering and death.

40. The distinctions of the "right hand" and the "left hand" are not to be passed out to companions as favors. Such reward must go to them "for whom it is prepared," that is, to the ones who procure it by faithfulness in life and administration.

42. This grieved display of narrow-minded desire turned into an event for the Lord to re-emphasize the way of genuine greatness (cf. 9:35). Initially, he helped the Twelve to remember the world's standard of greatness. It is standard for rulers and dignitaries to "exercise lordship" and "authority" over the general population.

43. Be that as it may, this must not be the custom among the followers of Christ. Interestingly, the person who might "be great" must be a "minister" to the people.

45. Jesus himself was the supreme example of one who showed genuine greatness. He who was God's Messiah ("Son of man;" see on 2:10) may well have attested his privilege "to be ministered unto" by men. Rather, he came to serve and "give his life" to humankind. "A ramson." This huge word was basic in the Greek universe of Jesus' day, where it was utilized to allude to the value paid to free a slave (Deissman, 1908).

This was the cost requested by a blessed God together that equity may be fulfilled in the absolution of sins. Therefore, in this installment, the adherent is liberated from transgression and Satan. "For some." The Greek relational word hostile to is all the more precisely deciphered in the place of, as overpowering proof from Greek sources illustrates (cf. Moulton and Milligan, 1995).

The Healing Of Blind Bartimaeus (10:46-52)

This section tells how Jesus, with his disciples, originated from Perea over the Jordan to

Jericho in Judea, where he restored the sight of Bartimaeus, the last healing supernatural occurrence of his public ministry.

46. The "Jericho" of Jesus' day was situated around five miles west of Jordan and fifteen miles upper east of Jerusalem. The site of the Canaanite city of Joshua's day lay one mile toward the north. There is a trouble in harmonization here. Matthew and Mark say that the supernatural occurrence happened as Jesus "left Jericho;" Luke places it "as he was come near unto Jericho (18:35).

Maybe the most conceivable arrangement is that the mending happened as Jesus left the site of old Jericho and entered the new city of Jericho. The trouble with this clarification is that there is no proof that the old Jericho was occupied in Jesus' time.

This issue emerges, most likely, from our absence of finished recorded and land data. We might be guaranteed that no disparity would exist if every one of the actualities were known. In the meantime, the difference is a declaration of the free character of the two records.

47. The blind beggar, by calling Jesus the "son of David," was remembering Him as Messiah. The conviction that the Messiah would be a relative of David was normal among the Jews of that day.

48. "Charged him." Many continued summoning (Gr. text) him to be quiet. He, be that as it may, continued crying all the more. He declined to be quieted.

49. "Be of good comfort." The verb intends to be of good cheer, to be gallant. It was just as they stated, "Brighten up!"

50. The verbs of this verse propose with what flurry Bartimaeus reacted to the call. He diverted from his shroud, bounced up ("rose," AV), and "came to Jesus." This was the chance of a lifetime, and it must not be permitted to disappear.

51. "Lord." The Aramaic word rabbouni was utilized by Mary Magdalene at the Resurrection (Jn. 20:16). It was a term of high regard, a fortified type of "rabbi," consolidating, in some measure, the implications of teacher and of Lord.

52. The healing was in light of the man's "faith," illustrated, as it seemed to be, by his relentless excitement, by his acknowledgment of Jesus as Messiah, and by the term rabbouni. The verb anablepo ("receive ... sight") intends to have locate reestablished, showing that the man had not always been visually impaired (blind).

"Made thee whole." the Greek word is sozo, signifying "to save," a term regularly utilized as a part of the Gospels to allude to physical recuperating and healing. It might be reworded, "Your faith has healed you."

Chapter Eleven

Christ's Concluding Ministry In Jerusalem
(11:1-13:37)

In this segment, Mark recorded the last demonstrations and lessons of the Savior before his energy. These occasions occurred in and around Jerusalem. Here happened the "Triumphal Entry' and the purifying (cleansing) of the Temple (11:1-26), the various debates with Jewish pioneers (11:27-12:44), and the broadened prophetically catastrophic talk on the Mount of Olives (13:1-37).

The Entrance Into Jerusalem And The Temple (11:1-26)

Starting here on, Christ surrendered the mindful state of mind that had made him pull back from territories of pressure and conceivable emergency. Presently, he tested the Jewish pioneers. In the passage into Jerusalem, he transparently incited objection and restriction. This "Triumphal Entry" ought to be seen not as the happening to a glorious king but rather as the introduction of a Savior who was soon to endure.

1. Comparison with Jn. 12:1 uncovers that Jesus started things out at "Bethany," where he spent the night. At that point, on the day after the Sabbath, he made his passageway into "Jerusalem." Bethany lay somewhat less than two miles toward the southeast of Jerusalem, not a long way from the eastern slant of "the Mount of Olives."

The area of Bethphage is more troublesome however the best confirmation appears to indicate a place at the foot of the eastern slant. Check's request is to switch the bearing taken by Jesus; however, he is reviewing the areas of the towns from the point of view of Jerusalem, which is said first.

John gives an explanation for trusting that Jesus landed in Bethany on Friday (12:1). The excursion to Jerusalem was more than a Sabbath day's adventure. It is accepted that Christ spent Saturday in Bethany and that the "Triumphal Entry' happened on Sunday.

2. "The village" was Bethphage, as Matt. 21:1 clarifies. "Over against you." That is, "opposite you." Whether Jesus knew about the yearling by past perception or by heavenly discernment is not clarified.

3. It gives the idea that he expected that the proprietor of the colt would know who "the Lord" was and would loan the creature to him. The favored Greek writings read, and immediately he will send it here again, a guarantee with respect to Jesus to give back the creature. Matthew expresses that there were two creatures, an ass and a yearling (21:2).

7. The "garments" set on the colt were external shrouds or robes, the splendid shades of which would give the foal the presence of bearing the accessories of eminence.

8. Others spread their robes "in the way," making an illustrious cover for the procession. Still others brought leaves, which they scattered on the way. John depicts them as palm branches (12:13).

9. The group encompassed the Lord; some "went before" him, and others "followed." And

they continued crying, "Hosanna." This is a transliteration of a Hebrew expression significance, Save I pray, originating from Ps. 118:25. It had turned into a term of acclaim and recognition and, in addition, a supplication to offer assistance. "Blessed be he that cometh..." is a correct citation from the LXX of Ps. 118:26.

This was one of the Hallel Psalms sung regarding the Passover celebration, and it was along these lines, especially fitting as of now. That the crowd utilized the words in a Messianic sense is clarified by the following verse.

10. The general population felt that the Messianic "kingdom of....David" was going to be set up. "Hosanna in the highest" without a doubt signifies, "Save, now, thou who art in the highest heavens." It is a cry addressed to God himself.

11. "Jesus entered....into the temple." The word hieron alludes to the entire sanctuary (temple) complex, including the courts and yards. When he "looked round about," his eyes would definitely take in the corners of the cash

changers and of the dealers of doves, which were to be the objects of his dismay on the next day.

12. "On the morrow." That is, on Monday. In the wake of spending the night in Bethany, the Lord set out again for Jerusalem.

13. It was typical for the "fig tree" in the region of Jerusalem to start to advance new leaves in the last portion of March or early April, the season of the Passover.

This tree was clearly completely left out, in which case it ought to have had matured figs on it, in spite of the fact that the season of ready figs was in June.

That it was the leaves that made Jesus expect organic products is clarified by the Greek word deciphered, "happy" (AV). This is the inferential conjunction ara, signifying "therefore." Jesus saw the leaves at a separation and came to see "if accordingly, he may discover organic product (figs)."

15. This is the second cleansing of the Temple, not in any sense to be related to the first, which

happened at the earliest reference point of Christ's ministry (Jn. 2:13-17). The individuals who "sold and purchased, the cash changers," and those "that sold doves" were in the utilize of Annas and the high priestly family.

The creatures were sold for conciliatory purposes, and the cash changers traded regular money for the half-shekel, which was important to pay for the sanctuary imposed. Excessive rates, in any case, were charged.

17. Jesus' citation originates from Isa. 56:7, where the prophet pronounces God's house to be a "house of prayer," a place set apart for holy utilization. Not exclusively did the Lord blame them for contaminating the Temple by utilizing it for business, but he also called attention to the fact that they made unscrupulous pickups from the terribly uncalled-for costs they charged. "Den if thieves." Taken from Jer. 7:11.

20. "In the morning." This was Tuesday morning, and Christ was coming back to Jerusalem again for the day.

22. The main importance of the reviling of the fig tree, which the Gospels state, is to be found in these verses. Jesus utilized it, for instance, to show "faith in God." Any further typical significance is without Scriptural defense.

24. "Believe." A current state is basic, calling for determination proceeding with faith. "Receive." The superior original copy confirms he favors the aorist tense - you did receive. At the end of the day, we are to continue trusting that God has effectively given us our request.

25. "Forgive ....that your Father....may forgive you." Statements, for example, those that make God's absolution reliant on our pardoning, have been misconstrued as being lawful in nature. In any case, Christ does not deliver himself here to the unsaved but rather to his disciples, the individuals who have, as of now, gone into a saving relationship with himself.

The Forgiveness of which he talks is not the underlying criminological demonstration of absolution, which nullifies the blame of sin. It is somewhat the absolution of a father that re-establishes fellowship. The point here is that a disciple can't ask viably if an unforgiving soul has broken his fellowship with God.

The Final Controversies With The Jewish Leaders (11:27-12:44)

The level-headed discussions recorded in this segment all occurred on one occupied day - Tuesday of the energy week. They concerned the accompanying subjects: the wellspring of our Lord's authority (11:27-33), the story of the vineyard and the husbandmen (12:1-12), a question about tax collection (12:13-17), the resurrection (12:18-27; the greatest commandment (12:28-34); the Messiah's relationship to David (12:35-40). The segment closes with an account of the widow's gift of two mites (12:41-44).

27. "Come back again to Jerusalem." This was Tuesday morning. The remarks on the shriveled fig tree (vv. 20-25) were talked about while in transit to Jerusalem. "The chief priests." Technically, there was yet one esteemed high priest. However, the term had come to incorporate all the living ex-high

priests. For this situation, in any event, Annas, the father-in-law of the high priest, Caiaphas, would have been incorporated.

28. Their question were two in number: What kind (poia) of "authority" do you have? What is the wellspring of "this authority?" By "these things," the authorities alluded to Christ's cleansing of the Temple (cf. Jn. 2:18). It was said that the Temple could be cleansed just by the Sanhedrin, by a prophet, or by the Messiah.

30. "From heaven." In an endeavor to maintain a strategic distance from the utilization of the Divine name, the Jews frequently utilized the expression "heaven" when discussing God.

31-32. By answering this question, Jesus put these religious leaders on the horns of a situation. In the event that John's service was of divine origin, then they, as spiritual leaders, ought to have been the first to "believe him." If they had expressed that his service was of a human beginning, they would have decreased John to fraud, and this would have summoned the dismay of "the general population" against them.

Chapter Twelve

Jesus Speaks To Them By Parables
(12:1-44)

1. "Parables." That Jesus gave more than one illustration of this event is seen by a correlation with Matt. 21:28-32, where the tale of the wicked husbandmen (devilish farmers) is gone before that of the two children. The prologue to the illustration, as found in Mk. 12:1 is unmistakeably drawn from Isa. 5:1,2.

The way that the vineyard there was representative of Israel (Isa. 5:7) provided the Jewish pioneers the insight for deciphering the parable of Jesus. "Hedge." The word utilized by Mark implies fence; it might have been a stone fence or divider. The "place for the wine fat" was a pit or trough underneath the winepress with the end goal of getting the juice.

The "tower" was a blend of a watchtower and storage place. The husbandmen were ranchers (farmers), and for this situation, vine producers were utilized here to speak to the religious leaders of Israel, for example, those being tended to by Jesus (cf. 11:27; 12:12).

2. The "servant," as in 12:4,5, represents a prophet whom God sent to Israel.

3. The way that they "caught" and "beat him" is demonstrative of the mistreatment of the prophets of the OT (cf. Matt. 23:34, 37).

6. "One son, his well-beloved." These words are an undeniable depiction of Christ himself (cf. 1:11; 9:7). The term "reverence" is excessively solid. Regard or give notice to is more precise.

7-8. The plot to "kill him" was a portrayal of the conspiring in which the Jewish pioneers were locked at that very time, keeping in mind the end goal to execute Jesus.

The forecast that the proprietor would "wreck the farmers" (destroy the husbandmen)" was satisfied in A.D. 70, when the Romans under Titus annihilated Jerusalem and put a conclusion to any similarity of self-control or self-rule which the Jews had already delighted in. The "others" unto whom the vineyard was to be given are additionally depicted in Matt. 21:43, where Jesus is cited as saying, "The kingdom of God might be taken from you, and given to a nation bringing forth the fruits thereof." This is an undeniable reference to the Gentiles and the Church.

10. The question, "Have ye not read," is stated to expect a positive answer. The citation in this verse and the following refer verbatim to the LXX of Ps. 118:22, 23. "The stone" is Christ, who was dismissed by "the builders," the religious leaders of the Jews.

13. In 12:13-17, "the Pharisees" and the Herodians address Jesus concerning the installment of tribute to Caesar. This mix is abnormal, for the Pharisees had a litter in the same manner as the Herodians. The previous was unalterably restricted to any remote overlordship, while the letter was supporters of the outside administration of the Herods.

The one gathering would have protested the Roman expense; the other would have favored it. The intention of these indistinguishable schemers was ulterior. They looked for "to got him in his words" as a seeker gets his prey.

14. "Carest for no man." This was proposed to be taken in a complimentary sense, implying

that his education was not affected by what companions or adversaries thought. The "tribute" was a survey assessment that must be paid by and into the Roman treasury. "Is it legal?" They needed him to answer concerning the equitable or unsoundness of the duty according to God.

15. "Why tempt ye me?" The master (Jesus) saw the difficulty into which they tried to draw him. They suspected that on the off chance that he replied in the agreed, the Jewish individuals who abhorred the survey duty would ascend and dismiss him and his cases; yet in the event that he answered in the negative, he could be accused of resistance to Rome. "A penny." This coin was the denarius with which the duty must be paid.

17. "Render." The verb intends to fork over the required funds. It expects an obligation to "Caesar." For the benefits given by the Roman government, the general population was obligated to help bolster that administration (cf. Rom. 13:1-7). By a similar token, they were additionally to pay their commitments to God. What's more, there is no confusion in

paying the two obligations, for both installments are for the achievement of God's will.

Such an answer totally disintegrated the foreseen problem, with the outcome that the examiners were totally astounded ("wondered, exetaumazon a strengthened word for great astonishment).

18. The topic of "the Sadducess" (vv. 18-27) actually concerned the "resurrection," which Jesus instructed, and they denied. For the Sadducees, there was no such thing as presence after death. They likewise precluded the truth from securing blessed messengers and spirits (Acts 23:8).

19. "Moses wrote." A free proclamation of the levirate law of marriage is found in Deut. 25:5-10. On the off chance that a man kicked the bucket without youngsters, his sibling was to wed his significant other, and the main child of that union was then viewed as the offspring of the dead spouse.

23. The issue which is raised appears to be unanswerable. "In the resurrection.... whose

spouse should she be ....?" The likelihood of a revival is just expected by the Sadducees as a reason for their contention. The motivation behind the question was to endeavor to demonstrate the inconceivability of a restoration by diminishing it to a ridiculousness.

24. "Err." The Greek verb intends to lead off track, to lead astray. They were being driven off track (or they were driving themselves off track) for two reasons. One, they didn't comprehend what the OT Scriptures instructed concerning restoration (cf. vv. 26, 27). Two, they thought little of "the power of God" to raise the dead and to determine all appearing challenges associated with the possibility of a resurrection.

25. With this one proclamation of reality, Jesus cleared away their evident issue. They had incorrectly accepted the continuation of marriage connections after the resurrection. Rather, Christ clarified that individuals will have indistinguishable relations from "the angels." There will be no requirement for marital union or the generation of children.

26. The question, "Have ye not read," expects an option reply, for Christ knew well that these Sadducees were completely comfortable with the Pentateuch. He alluded particularly to Exod. 3:6, citing the LXX.

27. The reality shown here is the reality of indecency. To be the God of Abraham is to be in cooperation with Abraham. It is subsequently unrealistic to be "the God of the dead" yet just "of the living." Thus, when God stood up from the burning bush, however, the patriarchs had been dead for a considerable length of time, and he was still in partnership with them. The contention of Christ then accepts that since there is life after death, this is adequate to demonstrate that resurrection will follow. Consummate human presence requests the union of the soul with the body.

28. The question concerning the chief commandment (vv. 28-34) originated from "one of the scribes." He was probably a Pharisee, for he affirmed Jesus' response to the Sadducees. There is, by all accounts, no ulterior rationale in this request (cf. vv. 28,32-34).

29-30. Jesus does not go to the traditions of the scribes for his answer; instead, he goes to the composed Law, to Deut. 6:4,5. The citation is taken from the LXX, with the expansion of the words "and with all thy mind." The "mind" and the "heart" are truly one and the same in Hebrew thought.

The words, "Hear O Israel; The Lord our God is one Lord," are from the statement of faith known as the "Shema" and are presented day by day by ardent Jews. It states the unmistakable standard of Hebrew confidence, that "God is one." The importance of this order to "love the Lord" is that he is to be loved with every one of man's powers and capabilities. This is the establishment and the rundown (summary) of man's total obligation to God.

31. "The second" rule is cited verbatim from Lev. 19:18 (LXX). Here, moreover, is the premise and the entirety of man's commitment to man. These two precepts are foundational to the lessons of all the Law and the Prophets (Matt. 22:40).

34. "Discreetly." That is, with insight, with intelligence. Christ pronounced the man to have the sort of profound understanding which, if continued in, would lead him into "the kingdom of God." The present, spiritual kingdom, which is entered by faith and new birth, is a top priority here (cf. Jn. 3:3,5).

Mark shuts his record of this discourse with a solid proclamation indicating how totally Christ had quieted his rivals. "No man" was setting out to question him anymore. Never again did they endeavor to trap Christ with a theological, philosophical, or lawful problem.

35. Be that as it may, Christ had not yet completed with his rivals. He had a question for them concerning the relationship of David to the Messiah (vv. 35-40). The reference to the instructing of "the scribes" speaks to the standard Jewish view that the Messiah would be a relative of David.

36. The citation is taken from Ps. 110:1 (LXX), a section that the Jews had been perceived as Messianic for quite a while. By first experience with the entry, Christ asserted the Davidic origin and also the awesome inspiration of the

Psalm. His motivation in utilizing David's words was to press home from the Scripture itself the reality of the deity of the Messiah.

37. The reality Jesus pointed up was that David called "him Lord." How, then, can the Messiah be both David's magnified Lord and his son? Matthew expresses that nobody could answer this question (22-46). However, remaining before them, the incarnate Son of God, Israel's Messiah, was himself the appropriate response represented. He was a relative of David "according to the flesh" and the Son of God "according to the spirit of holiness" (Rom. 1:3,4).

38. "Doctrine." Our pledge of "teaching" speaks to Mark's importance all the more precisely. "The long clothing" was the long streaming robe of a well-off individual or a dignitary. The "salutations" are clarified in Matt. 23:7.

39. The "uppermost rooms" are better portrayed as the seats (couches) of honor at meals (banquets).

40. Regardless of their acknowledgment as fair group leaders, the scribes were really blameworthy of the most terrible sort of deceptive nature, they made "long prayers" in the homes of widows to conceal the way that they were occupied with warped plans to deny them of their extremely "houses."

Chapter Thirteen

The Olivet Apocalypse (13:1-37)

The Olivet Apocalypse happened on Tuesday after the finish of the controversies in the sanctuary (Temple) courts with the Jewish leaders. It might be separated into the accompanying divisions: the inquiries of the disciples (13:1-4); the conditions normal for this present age (13:5-13); the coming crisis (13:14-23); the second coming of Christ (13:24-27); instruction concerning watchfulness (13:28-37).

1. In the light of Josephus' portrayals of the Temple, it is not amazing to discover one of the pupils shouting about the way of the stones and the structures. Josephus delineates the stones as being thirty-seven by twelve by eighteen feet in size.

He additionally expresses that the ".....front was all of cleaned stone, insomuch that its wellness, to, for example, had not seen it, was unbelievable, and to, for example, had seen it, was significantly astonishing" (Antiq. XV, xi. 3-5, Josephus,2012).

2. Jesus utilized the solid Greek twofold negative development (ou me) twice in this verse so as to deny that "one stone" would be left "upon another." It was decidedly sure that the Temple would be totally crushed (destroyed), a reality affirmed by history when in A.D. 70 under Titus, the Temple, alongside the city, was laid in remnants.

4. "These things." A conspicuous reference to the forecast expressed in 13:2. There is motivation to accept, in any case, that the followers likewise needed to mind the arrangement of end-time occasions. Their second question opened up the first in that it requested the sign which would demonstrate that satisfaction was about (melle) to happen. From Matthew, we discover that the supporters additionally solicited concerning the sign of Christ's coming and of the finish of the age (24:3).

5. Jesus started his answer by envisioning the conditions character of this present age (vv. 5-13). The first is the presence of deceivers, against whom the disciples must "take heed" continually (Gr. pres. imper.).

6. "In my name." These words allude to the happening to false saviors (false messiahs), who will guarantee the position and authority that have a place with Christ alone. The prediction was satisfied with various events. Maybe the most remarkable personage making such a claim was Bar Cochba (A.D. 132).

8. Wars are normal for the whole age, as they seem to be "earthquakes" and "famines." "Troubles" is overlooked by the better Greek original copies. These conditions are portrayed as "the beginnings of sorrows."

Accordingly, they are set in direct difference to the end (v.7). "Sorrows" really implies birth-torments, a term utilized by the Jews to depict the torments and troubles that are to introduce (usher in) the happening to the Messiah.

9. The disciple is told to "take heed," that is, to be always on the alert (Gr. pres. imper.). "Councils." Literally sanhedrins. The captures, arrests, and beatings anticipated here start to discover their fulfillment in the book of Acts (cf. 4:5 ff; 5:27 ff.), as do likewise the appearances "before rulers and kings" (cf. 12:1 ff.; 24:1 ff; 25:1 ff). These appearances were to

be "for a testimony" to them (autois), not against them, as in the AV. Consider Paul's observer to Felix (Acts 24:24,25) and Agrippa (Acts 26).

10. Another component of the age is the overall proclaiming (preaching) of "the gospel." The end (v.7) can't come until the evangelistic task has "first" been refined. Matthew 24:14 closes the idiom with the statement, "Then shall the end come," alluding to the end of the age.

13. Amidst every one of the aggravations, the ethical declension, and the abuses, endurance turns into the mark of spiritual genuineness .. "The end." Since the conditions portrayed in 13:5-13 are age-long, "the end" does not here allude to the end of the age, but instead to the end of life or of the trial.

"Be saved." In this setting, physical deliverance can't be implied. The promise is that the person who endures shall be saved spiritually. The endurance, be that as it may, is not the premise of salvation. With regards to the general instructing of the NT, endurance is to be seen as the consequence of the new birth (cf. Rom. 8:29-39; I Jn. 2:19).

A man who has been regenerated and in this way persists (endures), without a doubt, experiences the fulfillment of salvation.

14. Having called attention to a portion of the remarkable components of this age, Christ went ahead to depict the coming crisis (vv. 14-23). The " abomination of desolation" is an expression taken verbatim from Dan. 12:11 (LXX). It is likewise found with slight varieties in Dan. 9:27; 11:31.

Among the Jews, the expression "abomination" was utilized to portray worshipful admiration (idolatry) or blasphemy (sacrilege) (cf. Ezk. 8:9,10,15,16). It appears to be, along these lines, that both Daniel and Christ were discussing a shocking profanation of the Temple. The principal satisfaction of Daniel's prophetic utilization of the term, a few authors claim, was the erection of an adjustment to Zeus on the sacred place of burnt offering at the command of Antiochus Epiphanes in 168 B.C.

Christ's utilization of the words had quick reference to the profanation of the Temple by the Romans (A.D. 70). It must be recalled that the disciples had solicited concerning the annihilation of the Temple (Mk. 13:2,4). Moreover, the guidelines given in 13:14b-18 appear to fit that event best.

In any case, the nearby connection of these conditions to Christ's second appearance (vv. 24-27) requests an extra application to the season of the end. The conditions of the times of Antiochus Epophanes and of the Roman demolition of the Temple were foreshadowings of the times of the Antichrist promptly before Christ's arrival (cf. II Thess. 2:3,4; Rev. 13:14,15).

"Standing where it ought not." In the holy place (Matt. 24:15). The presence of the horrifying profanation would be an indication for tenants in Judea to "flee to the mountains" with a specific end goal to keep away from the coming attack. The particular reference of this order, and in addition to those in verses 15-18, was to the soon-coming destruction of Jerusalem (A.D. 70).

15-16. The requirement for flurry (to take haste) would be urgent to the point that there would be no opportunity to delay "to take anything" for the flight.

17-18. It would be an extremely troublesome time for expectant mothers and those with babies in arms. A flight "in the winter" would add to the challenges of an officially troublesome circumstance.

19. This outline depiction of the tribulations of "those days" is surely connected to the repulsions of A.D. 70, as a correlation with Josephus' Wars of the Jews (Preface, 4; V, VI) will appear. Be that as it may, there is motivation to trust that Christ looked past Roman days to the considerable last tribulation, which will go before his second coming. This is recommended by the words "neither shall be," which are an interpretation of a solid Greek dissent (ou me).

20. It is impractical to point this verse to the proposed clarifications in light of such an impediment is acceptable. There are components here that go past that time and are all the more accurately connected with the finish of the age. The reference to 'the choose' appears to indicate the spared amid the times

of the Great Tribulation only before Christ's arrival. For their purpose, God has "shortened the days" of that time of terrible, horrendous affliction.

22. So striking will these deceivers be that they will expect to lead astray" even the elect." However, the provision, "if it were possible" demonstrates that it is unimaginable, unthinkable, that they ought to succeed. On the recognizable proof of "the elect," see Lk. 18:7; Rom. 8:33; Col. 3:12; I Pet. 1:2.

24-25. The prophecy now proceeds onward to the Second Advent (vv. 24-27). Christ particularly put this extraordinary occasion "in those days after that tribulation,"obviously alluding to the time portrayed in 13:14-23. This requires one of two clarifications.

Either Christ was to come not long after A.D. 70 or the afflictions of verses 14-23 have a twofold reference, both to the obliteration of Jerusalem by Titus and to the Great Tribulation toward the end of the age. Since the previous clarification is outlandish, the last translation is seen as the way to the comprehension of the part all in all.

The dialect used to depict the disturbances in the heavens is to a great extent, taken from the OT (cf. Isa. 13:10; 34:4; Joel 2:10,30,31). While it is best to maintain a strategic distance from an extraordinary peculiarity here, there is no purpose behind not understanding these expressions to allude to real celestial changes that will promptly go before Christ's coming. It is not at all strange that such a groundbreaking event ought to be presented in this way.

26. This is the individual, substantial return of Christ to the earth "with incredible power and glory," which is depicted in such entries as Acts 1:11; II Thess. 1:7-10; 2:8; Rev. 1:7; 19:11-16. "Against the foundation of an obscured paradise, the Son of Man is uncovered in the Shekinah magnificence of God. . . . ." (Beasley-Murray, 1957). The dialect utilized here is drawn from Dan. 7:13. "They shall see." His coming will be noticeable to all men.

27. Now the resurrection of the righteous dead and the transformation of the living holy people will happen (cf. I Cor. 15:51-53; I Thess. 4:13-18).

Then "he shall gather together his elect," the redeemed of all ages, at various times (past & present). Concerning the word "elect," see on 13:22.

The word episynaxei, "gather together," is the verb type of the noun episynagoge, "gathering together," in II Thess. 2:1. They will be accumulated to the slipping Lord from all parts of the earth ("the four winds"), even from the most distant furthest points ("farthest piece of the earth" and "of heaven").

28-29. Having completed the outline of future events, the Lord swung to an exchange of the requirement for watchfulness (vv.28-37). There is no sign that Israel is symbolized here by the fig tree. Rather, the story is a straightforward showing of reality that coming events cast their shadows before them. At the point when these things start to happen, we will realize that the consumption is extremely near. The "things" to which Christ alludes are the events portrayed in verses 14-25.

30. The most common clarification of the expression "this generation" is that it alludes to the era of individuals alive when Christ was

talking. Amid their lifetime, every one of these things were to happen in the pulverization of Jerusalem in A.D. 70. This occasion is utilized by Christ as a preparatory picture prefiguring, in all its fundamental qualities, the end of the age (cf. Mk. 9:1).

32. The correct "day" and "hour" of Christ's arrival are not humanly perceivable. Indeed, time is known only by God the Father. The announcement that "the Son" did not know the season of the culmination is to be comprehended in the light of his self-constraint amid the times of his humiliation (cf. Phil. 2:5-8). He had assumed a position of complete subjection to the Father, practicing his heavenly qualities just at the Father's offering (cf. Jn. 8:26,28,29).

33. "Take ye heed." This current state basically calls for steady readiness. The same is valid for the verb "watch," which intends to keep oneself conscious. Such watchfulness is fundamental since we don't know when these end-time occasions may break upon us.

35. The follower is to "watch" persistently (Gr. current state). This verb, and in addition that

in verse 33, intends to be or keep wakeful. It calls for consistent sharpness over rest or tiredness. "At even.... midnight.... cockcrowing ....morning." These are the four watches of the night, as indicated by the Roman retribution.

36. Such watchfulness is fundamental for fear that the Lord come when we don't expect him. This is what he implies by discovering us "dozing." To a man who is not watching, Christ's coming will be sudden. One who is on the ready will see the indications of the Lord's arrival (vv. 28,29) and won't be shocked.

Chapter Fourteen

Christ's Passion And Resurrection (14:1-16:20)

Treachery And Devotion (14:1-11)

Mark's story moves now into the last scenes of Christ's life on earth. These were the occasions that encompassed his death and resurrection. They were the demonstrations that would achieve redemption for all individuals wherever who would accept and receive it.

These verses start with a depiction of the foul play with which the priests and scribes plotted Jesus' death (vv. 1,2). Conversely, this is trailed by a moving record of Mary's commitment (vv. 3-9). At that point, in significantly more honed complexity, the Evangelist relates the traitorous plot of Judas to sell out the Lord (vv. 10,11).

1. "After two days." The point from which these two days were figured was presumably late Tuesday evening, at which time the Jewish leaders were looking for "how they may take him by craft." This would put the Passover feast on Thursday evening.

3. The time was Tuesday evening; Christ had come back to "Bethany" to spend the night. We don't know anything of "Simon the leper" past what is given in these verses, albeit some have erroneously distinguished him from Simon the Pharisee in Lk. 7:36-50.

"Sat at meat." That is, leaned back on a loveseat at the table. The woman of the story was Mary, the sister of Martha (cf. Jn. 12:2,3). The "alabaster box" was a flask with a long neck that was severed, keeping in mind the end goal of utilizing the substance. "Ointment of spikenard." The Greek content is best interpreted as certified nard. The Nard plant was utilized to make perfume. "Very Precious." The cost was around fifty-five dollars for a pound (cf. v.5).

5. "Three hundred pence." That is three hundred denarii. This was a Roman silver coin worth around eighteen pennies. "They murmured." The verb utilized here communicates a forceful feeling, initially intending to grunt. A more expressive interpretation would be they started to scold her extremely.

8. He clarified the genuine explanation behind Mary's activity. The deed was not only a demonstration of commitment but rather a cognizant goal to "anoint" Christ in suspicion of his moving toward death and internment. Since Mary had sat at the feet of Jesus and listened eagerly to his lessons, she had come to see, far and away superior to the disciples, the reality of his coming death.

10. Judas' response to the reproach of Jesus was traitorous. An entire examination of the man's thought processes in going "unto the chief priests" is unrealistic with our constrained information. Luke clarifies it by saying that "Satan entered" into him (22:3). We realize that his adoration for cash was a fractional explanation behind the treachery (cf. Matt. 26:14,15).

It is likewise conceivable that he had been frustrated by Christ's inability to ascend against Rome and build up a free Jewish kingdom.

11. The measure of cash they "promised to give him" was thirty bits of silver (Matt. 26:15), which would be worth in the vicinity of twenty and twenty-five dollars. "He sought."

Continuing activity (Greek blemished tense). From this time on, Judas continually searched for the correct minute to "betray him."

The Lord's Passion *(14:12-15:47)*

Mark's record of Christ's suffering and death might be plotted as follows: the occasions encompassing the last dinner (14:12-25), the trip to Gethsemane (14:26-42), the capture (14:43-52); the trials (14:53-15:15); the torturous killing (15:16-41); the internment (15:42-47).

The typical order expects that Wednesday was spent as a day of rest in Bethany and that the occasions of the segment under thought happened on Thursday and Friday. It is not unequivocally expressed that such a day of rest is mediated, yet a correlation of the Gospel records makes it important to accept that it did.

12. The "first day of unleavened bread" may, at first believed, be taken to be the day after the Passover, or Nisan 15 (cf. Lev. 23:5,6). In any case, Mark makes it plain that he is alluding to

Nisan 14; he says it was "the point at which they killed the Passover" (cf. Exod. 12:6).

It is realized that the Feast of Unleavened Bread was viewed as starting upon the arrival of the Passover. This was Thursday. The Passover meal would have been eaten after sun-down on the start of Nisan 15.

14. Having taken after the servant to the house, the disciples were to make their demand of "the goodman of the house" (Greek, master of the house, householder). Who the proprietor was is not known. Some have proposed that the house was that of Mark. However, this is theory.

The Greek content peruses, Where is my visitor chamber? It appears from the utilization of the pronoun that the Lord had beforehand made courses of action for the utilization of the room. "Eat the Passover." Some, on the premise of specific explanations in John's Gospel, assume that the supper was not the Passover but rather one preceding the Passover (cf. Jn.13:1,29; 18:28; 19:14,31).

In any case, unmistakably, Mark speaks to Christ with the aim of eating the Passover. Besides, the announcements in John don't really request the view that the Last Supper went before the season of the Passover (Robertson,1950).

16. Not exclusively did Christ plan to eat the Passover, but Mark particularly expresses that the followers "made prepared" the Passover. This would incorporate the slaughtering and simmering of the sheep and the arrangement of the other recommended things.

17. "At night." The Passover was eaten after nightfall (sunset) on the start of the fifteenth of Nisan.

19. The question, "Is it I? expected an answer in the negative and might be deciphered. It is not I, is it? So gigantic a wrongdoing appeared to be mind-blowing to the eleven. Matthew says (26:25) that Judas likewise posed the question; however, this was clearly an endeavor to shroud his treachery.

20. "In the dish." To eat together, and particularly to share the substance of the

regular bowl, was an indication of warm fellowship. In the light of this custom, Judas' arranged selling out is uncovered as still more deplorable.

21. "As it is written." See 1:2. The OT entry to which Jesus had reference would appear to be one that portrays his disloyalty (his betrayal), maybe Ps. 41:9. See that God's sovereign reason, communicated in the words, "it is written," did not in the least free Judas of good duty regarding his demonstration.

22. At the Passover dinner, the "bread" that Jesus utilized would have been the unleavened cakes endorsed for the devour. When Jesus stated, "This is my body," he clearly signified, "This symbolizes my body." His physical body was as yet present with them. This is like the symbolic utilization, which happens in Jn. 6:35; 8:12; 10:9. The same is valid for his announcement concerning his blood (Mk. 14:24).

23. "The cup." We have no chance to get to know which of the four Passover mugs Jesus utilized. Regardless, in any case, the substance

would have been wine blended with 66% water.

24. "The New Testament." In both Matthew and Mark, the best Greek writings discard the word "new." However, see Lk. 22:20; I Cor. 11:25. While the Greek word "diatheke" may allude to a confirmation or will, the OT foundation of Christ's comment requests the interpretation, pledge (cf. Exod. 24:8). This is not the term used to express an understanding between equivalent gatherings (syntheke). God alone started the terms of the contract, and man could just acknowledge or reject it.

The blood of Christ is the blood of the new covenant promised in Jer. 31:31-34 (cf. Heb. 8:6-13). "For many." While the Greek relational word, hyper may signify instead of," it is utilized commonly to signify "rather than." This is one of the clearest confirmations that Jesus saw his passing as vicarious (Taylor,1953).

25. "No more." A solid disavowal implying that Jesus would in no way, shape, or form any more drink with them amid this present age. The "kingdom of God" in this comment is eschatological, presumably alluding to the

relationship in the Millennial kingdom to be set up when Christ returns (Rev. 20:4-6).

26. The "hymn," as indicated by Passover use, would have been a bit of the Hallel Psalms (Ps. 115-118). The trip to the Garden of Gethsemane on "the mount of Olives" and Christ's three sessions of petition are recorded in 14:26-42.

27. "Be offended." The word was initially intended to get in a trap or catch. It came to allude, likewise, to the demonstration of making somebody stagger or stumble. Jesus stated, along these lines, that the occasions of that night would surprise every one of them and end up being a catch or a stumbling block.

"Because of me this night." Omitted by some of the most huge Greek compositions. "It is composed." See 1:2. The citation is taken from Zech. 13:7, being unreservedly interpreted from the Hebrew content.

30. Christ focused on the promptness of the event - "this day .... this night." Also he tended to Peter with the determined individual pronoun, "thou." Of the considerable number

of followers, Peter, however, demanded his faithfulness and would "deny the Lord."

No disagreement is to be envisioned with alternate Gospels concerning the quantity of times the "cockerel" was to "crow." The others simply express the way that the foreswearing would precede chicken crowing (the third watch of the night; see 13:35). Stamp includes details by saying the particular number of times that the chicken would crow.

31. "He spake." Peter over and over avowed his boast, and he did as such unequivocally (intensely). "In any wise." A magnificent interpretation of the Greek twofold negative, ou me, which communicates solid refusal. With this, the majority of the followers continued concurring.

33. "Sore amazed." A solid word, communicating profound, passionate bombshell and pain. It has been interpreted in different courses (to be totally disturbed, to be alarmed, horrified, profoundly fomented). Mark adds to this expression, "very heavy" (ademonein), which talks about bewilderment and distress.

34. Jesus was distressed and grieved to the very point of "death." Hence, he requests that they "watch" "to stay awake, conscious, caution, and attentive."

35. "The hour" concerning which Jesus prayed was the time when, in the arrangement of God, he was to endure and bite the dust as an atonement for sin (cf. Jn. 12:23,27; 13:1).

36. "Abba" is the Aramaic word for "father." "This cup" alludes to indistinguishable things from "the hour" (v. 35). It was the measure of torment and death which were more than physical. The desolation from which the Lord shrank was the anguish of the soul coming about because of bearing the blame of a lost world.

The affliction was to be profound and enduring, a partition from God the Father (cf. Mk. 15:34). Also, it was concerning that Christ asked that the cup be evacuated on the off chance that it was workable for God to achieve his redemptive reason by some different means. By and by, he was in flawless accommodation with the Father, wanting his will alone.

38. Here, the Lord adds the command to "pray" all together that they may not "enter into temptation." This threat must be translated as particularly alluding to the coming testings related to the Lord's arrest and death.

40. "Heavy." Literally, their eyes were weighted down with rest. The early English word "wist" implied knew. They had no excuse.

41. He came to them "the third time" after praying once more yet (Matt. 26:44). it is hard to know in what sense Jesus implied the comment concerning sleeping and resting. Some take it as a question (RSV); others find in it a " kind of sad bitterness: (Gould, 1948, 2016). Since he had risen up out of the darkness of the hour, he at no time in the future required the assurance that they were in some sense confronting the trial with him.

This is by all accounts. The idea behind the words "It is enough." "Is betrayed." The current state, which ought to be interpreted as being sold out, implies that the disloyalty and betrayal were occurring at that exact second.

43. The accompanying verses (43-52) relate the capture of Christ. The mob was driven by "Judas," who realized that Jesus frequently resigned to the seclusion of Gethsemane (Jn. 18:2). The huge number incorporated a portion of the Roman companion garrisoned in Jerusalem and additionally the sanctuary (Temple) police (Jn. 18:3). Doubtlessly the warriors were apprehensive "with swords" and the sanctuary police with "staves" (clubs).

The "chief priests, the scribes, and the elders" were the three gatherings of which the Sanhedrin was made, demonstrating that the capturing (arresting party) had been formally dispatched by the body.

45. "Judas," in derided regard, filled the role of a dependable follower, welcoming his teacher as "Master" (Gr., rabbi) and afterward kissing him intensely. The Greek verb for the last demonstration is a fortified type of the word interpreted as "kiss" in verse 44. By this strengthened demonstration of ridicule dedication, Judas just added to his blame.

48. Christ reproached them for regarding him as if he were an equipped looter or outlaw (thief, AV).

49. The capture in an off the beaten path put under the front of haziness was altogether superfluous since he had been "in the temple instructing" each day. By this dissent, Christ brought up the craziness of their methodology, which undermined their purpose behind capture and trial.

However, God had anticipated their activities and the course of occasions in the "scriptures" (for instance, cf. Isa. 53:8,9,12). In this way, paying little heed to the rationale of Christ's dissents, the capture would be issued in trial, and the trial would be executed.

51. "A certain young man." The Greek word neaniskos was utilized for men between twenty-four and forty years old. No other Gospel records this occurrence. Thus, we have no additional data concerning the individual's personality. It has frequently been proposed, maybe effectively, that Mark was making a hidden reference to himself. There is, by all

accounts, no other explanation as to why this irrelevant occasion was incorporated.

52. "Naked." The word gymnos does not really mean exposed; it was additionally used to portray a man dressed just in underwear (undergarment).

53. Here, the record swings to the Jewish and Roman trials of Christ (14:53-15:15). Check moves instantly to the record of the night trial before the Sanhedrin (vv. 53-65). The analyzing body was the Sanhedrin, which appeared by the nearness of "all the chief priests and the elders and the scribes. The high priest, as of now, was Caiaphas.

54. Maybe on the grounds that he was resolved to satisfy his brag of steadfastness, "Peter followed" Jesus. Be that as it may, fear held him at a distance, and thus, he was not ready to slip into the place of the high priest with the group. Mark's statement interpreted "palace" as aulen and really alludes to a courtyard.

John clarifies (18:15, 16) that another disciple secured a passage for Peter. "The servants" with whom "he sat" were most likely temple police and chaperons of the high priest.

55. The word interpreted as "council" is synedrion, from which "sanhedrin" comes. They carried on a delayed hunt (ezetoun) for observers against Jesus. These individuals from the Jewish court were going about as prosecutors.

58-59. These people were discussing Christ's comment amid his initial Judean service on the event of the primary cleansing of the Temple (Jn. 2:19). The deception of their witness' was confirmed by their abuse of the announcement and by their inability to concur.

60. Humiliated by the contradiction of the witness, "the high priest" endeavored to include Christ in the exchange, clearly trusting that his answer would demonstrate his blame.

61. The question, "Art thou the Christ?" puts the individual pronoun in the insistent position; it might be rendered, You, will be you the Messiah? It was regular for the Jews to utilize some such term as the "Blessed" when alluding to God altogether. They would wind

up noticeably liable for maligning the perfect name.

Matthew makes it clear (26:63) that the high priest put Jesus under a serious pledge (an oath), which made it compulsory for him to reply. He had no chance to get out; however, he had to hold up under a witness who would betray him.

62. With a frank affirmation, Jesus replied, "I am." The rest of his answer is framed in wording taken from Dan. 7:13 and Ps. 110:1. The "right hand of power" is the right hand of God. Christ guaranteed his judges that the day would come when they would consider him to be the Messiah, practicing the power of God and coming in judgment (see 13:26).

63. This was the sort of answer sought by the high priest. He speedily "rent his garments," as he was required to do at the sound of blasphemy (Swete, 1953). No "further witnesses were required since Jesus had been compelled to bear witness against himself, an illegal procedure under Jewish law.

64. The statement of Christ was translated as "blasphemy" in light of the fact that the authorities saw Jesus as an insignificant man, a mere man (cf. Jn. 10:33). The subject of his blame was put to the whole council, and they collectively "condemned him to be guilty." The built-up punishment for blasphemy was death(Lev. 24:16).

65. Clearly it was "some" of the individuals from the Sanhedrin who started to treat Jesus in the despicable way portrayed. For such exceptionally set, regarded religious leaders of Judaism, the demonstrations of these dignitaries were generally debasing.

They covered "his face" with a blindfold when they struck him to make a joke of his supernatural knowledge (cf. Lk. 22:64). When he was swung over to "the servants" (the temple police), these took after the case of the authorities and started to "strike him." The word rapisma alludes either to a blow with a pole (rod) or to a slap with the palm of the hand.

67. "Looked upon him." The word demonstrates that she settled her look on him.

In view of John's intervention for Peter (Jn. 18:15, 16), the servant most likely was certain that Peter was a devotee of Jesus.

68. Peter's refusal was fortified by redundancy ("know not, neither understand it"). Caught by the sudden recognizable proof, he overlooked his boast of dependability. The "porch" to which Peter pulled back was the forecourt or vestibule driving from the road into the yard. Numerous old writings overlook the words "and the cock crew."

69. The Greek content shows this was the same "maid" who had beforehand blamed Peter, notwithstanding Matt. 26:71 discusses another housekeeper, while in Luke 22:58 states that someone else (manly) tended to Peter straightforwardly. It is not important to discover inconsistencies among the records here. There were apparently two servants, the doorkeeper and another, who guided Peter out toward the spectators. What's more, a name said to Peter, "You likewise are one of them."

70. The third allegation originated from a few people who remained by. There were most likely various proclamations made, as the

flawed tense elegon may well show. John 18:26 uncovers that one of those making allegations was a relative of the individual whose ear Peter had cut off.

71. "To curse and to swear." These verbs don't imply that Peter utilized irreverence as the term is seen today. Rather, he called down a "revile, a curse," most likely upon himself under oath in making his denial.

72. Here, the composition legitimizes the incorporation of the words "the second time" (see on v. 68). The best messages additionally contain "quickly" (euthys). The second of the cock followed after hard on the third foreswearing, striking profoundly into the awareness of the fallen supporter. In the meantime, Peter saw Jesus looking downward at him (Lk. 22:61) from a room over the patio. "He thought subsequently." The word epibalon has been an issue of interpretation here for some time.

Likely, the RSV rendering he broke down is ideal. Where epibalon portrays the onset of the sobbing and weeping, the imperfect tense eklaien, he wept, depicts the continuation of it.

Chapter Fifteen

The Lord's Passion Continued (15:1-47)

1. This verse depicts a moment meeting of the Sanhedrin at a young hour in the morning. Luke 22:66-71 gives a full record of this period of the Jewish trial. It seems to have been an endeavor to make the judgment legitimate since it was unlawful to hold a trial during the night.

As of now, the Romans did not allow the Jews to exact the sentence of the death penalty. Thus, it was important to take Jesus to "Pilate," who was the Roman procurator over Judea.

2. The Roman trial is portrayed in 15:2-15. For an entire record of the Roman trial, see Jn. 18:28-19:16. One of the charges was that Jesus asserted to be a "king," and it was out of this affirmation that Pilate's question developed. A claim to authority was grounds for trial for conspiracy.

Jesus answers, "Thou sayest," is fit for being differently translated notwithstanding, in the light of Jn. 18:34-38, it appears to be best to comprehend it as a positive answer, which, as

John shows, was joined by a clarification of what sort of a lord Jesus asserted to be.

3-4. These verses picture "the chief priests" as they tossed a torrent of allegations against Jesus. So horrible was the assault that "Pilate" couldn't comprehend the quiet disposition of the detainee (cf. v.5).

6. The governor had built up a routine with regards to discharging "one detainee" every year at the Passover, maybe as an endeavor to keep up the cooperative attitude of the Jews. The verbs "he released" and "they desired" (Greek, asked) are both in the defective tense, demonstrating that these were standard acts, i.e., "He used to release....."

7. The detainee "Barabbas" was no unimportant frivolous criminal. He was a burglar (Jn. 18:40), an insurrectionist, and a killer. It creates the impression that the man was a Jew who had partaken in an uprising against Rome, fundamentally the same as the wrongdoing to of which the Jews were denouncing Jesus (Gould, 2016).

8. "Crying so anyone might hear." The better old original copies read anabas, "went up" (ASV).

The group requested that Pilate play out his standard demonstration ("had ever done;") of discharging a detainee. It appears that the group was asking for the arrival of Barabbas, since he may well have been a sort of legend to them due to his part in the resistance to Rome.

11. Now, the group may have been enticed to ask for the arrival of Jesus. However, the ministers "moved the general population" to request Barabbas. The word anaseio signifies "to prompt, to mix up," or move actually, "to shake up," demonstrating the energized tumult of the horde.

15. "Willing to content the general population." The Greek expression (to hikanon poiesai) infers that he was ready to fulfill the Jews, regardless of the possibility that he needed to yield an innocent man to do it. "Scourged." This demonstration was refined with a whip made of portions of cowhide with harsh bits of metal tied at the finishes of the strips.

The casualty was twisted forward over a short post, and the discipline was managed to his exposed back. Frequently, the resultant profound slices opened the substance to the exceptional bone.

16. It was not yet 9:00 A.M. The trial before Pilate was taken after in the blink of an eye by the torturous killing (15:16-41). "The soldiers" to whom Jesus was conferred were the Roman military workforce under the purview of Pilate. "The hall." The Greek word is aule, "courtyard," the same as in 14:54, where it is interpreted as "royal residence" (AV).

Mark clarifies that it was "called Pretorium," a term which could well allude either to the royal residence of Herod or to the stronghold of Antonia, where the Roman troops were quartered.

At any rate, it appears to allude to the trooper's sleeping enclosure. The "band" was a Roman associate containing around six hundred men. Be that as it may, the figure changed with the circumstances, and in this example, it could have been a great deal less.

19. The three verbs, "smote, spit, and worshipped," are all in the imperfective tense, portraying the reiteration of these demonstrations. Many soldiers made a biting joke of Jesus' misjudged case to be a king.

21. John 19:17 clarifies that as the parade set out for the execution, Jesus was bearing his own particular cross. In a matter of seconds, be that as it may, the fighters happened upon "Simon" and constrained him to convey the instrument of execution. This current man's character was clearly known by Mark's Roman perusers, for Mark says his children, "Alexander and Rufus," as commonplace people. There was a Rufus in Rome when Paul composed the Epistle to the Romans (16:13).

22. "Golgotha" is an Aramaic word meaning a skull. The place was presumably so named by its shape. The conventional site still supported by many is the Church of the Holy Sepulcher. Others demand the slope known as Gordon's Calvary. In light of a legitimate concern for objectivity, we should concede that, right now, beyond any doubt, recognizable proof of the spot is unthinkable.

23. "Gave." The imperfective tense, edidoun, is better made an interpretation of they would give. Jesus rejected the drink in the wake of tasting it and finding what it was (Matt. 27:34). "Myrrh" filled in as a medication directed to stifle the torment of the terrible passing of torturous killing. Jesus, be that as it may, declined to permit such a stupifying elixir to cloud his mind.

24. The points of interest of the torturous killing are truant from the greater part of the Gospels. It is known from Jn. 20:25, nails were utilized to attach the hands to the cross. Torturous killing was perceived as being a standout amongst the most brutal types of execution utilized in the ancient world. Frequently the casualty was left on the cross for a few days before death assuaged his extreme enduring. The "pieces of clothing (garments)" of the sentenced man were left to the killers.

25. The season of the torturous killing is set at "the third hour," which was the Jewish assignment for 9:00 A.M. The trial before Pilate happened about the 6th hour,

concurring Roman time, which would be 6:00 A.M. (cf. Jn. 19:14).

26. It was standard to utilize a notice or some likeness thereof showing the name and the "allegation" of the censured man. Mark gives just the wrongdoing (accusations) of which Jesus was charged. John demonstrates that "the superscription" additionally contained the recognizable proof, "Jesus of Nazareth" (19:19). There is no disagreement; Mark is only more compact.

27. The two offenders executed with Jesus were more than simple frivolous "hoodlums." As in 14:48, lestes signifies "burglar, outlaw, robber."

29-30. "Railed on him." The passers by continued cursing (eblasphemoun) Jesus. "Swaying their heads." They shook their heads in hateful objection. The rationale behind their mockery was a contention from the more noteworthy to the lesser. In the event that he could remake the Temple in three days, positively, he could, without much of a stretch, "descend from the cross."

31. The "chief priests" and "the scribes" take an interest in the joke, however, among themselves. Their oft-rehashed mockery concerning Christ's failure to spare himself was in all actuality a disavowal that he could help anyone. On the off chance that he couldn't convey himself from torment and death, how might he be able to convey any other person?

33. Three hours had passed; it was presently twelve, "the 6th hour." At the hour of the sun's brightest light, "darkness" came (egeneto) "over the entire land." This couldn't have been an aggregate obscuration so that the entire earth was obscured (Lenski, 1951), for the Passover happened at the season of the full moon when no such overshadowing is conceivable.

What created the darkness is not expressed. Positively, the planning of the Marvel was supernatural. The "ninth hour" was 3:00 P.M. (see v. 25).

34. Jesus had been on the cross for six hours. His cry was a citation from Ps. 22:1. "Eloi, Eloi, lama sabachthani is a transliteration from Aramaic, the local tongue of Christ. Mark, as

his exclusively seemed to be, gave the significance of the Aramaic for his Roman perusers. This cry of deserting gives a look into the internal sufferings of Christ on the cross.

His most prominent anguish was not physical; it was fairly misery of the spirit, and he bore the blame for the world's transgression. The sense in which God had "neglected" Jesus Christ was that the Father pulled back from fellowship with the Son. At no time in the future did he confirm his affection toward his Son. Rather, Christ had turned into the question of the Father's dismay, for he was the heathen's (sinner's Substitute) Substitute. Christ progressed toward becoming "sin for us" (II Cor. 5:21), and a holy God can not look with favor upon sin.

36. The "vinegar" was a harsh wine that extinguished thirst more promptly than water. Since this was not a medicated blend as in verse 23, Jesus got it without dissent (cf. Jn. 19:29,30). "Regardless of whether Elias will come."

There is no explanation behind expecting that the speakers were true in their words. This was doubtlessly a continuation of the joke that is so clear in 15:29-32.

37. "Gave up the ghost." The Greek word is exepneusen, which actually implies that he inhaled out or lapsed. It was not a drawn-out battle, for example, the flawed tense would portray. Rather, the aorist tense delineates a short, flitting event. He inhaled out his soul and was gone.

38. "The veil" was the substantial drapery that isolated the Holy Place from the Holy of Holies in "the temple" (naos, "asylum"). For a depiction, see Josephus Wars of the Jews V. v.4. The lease moved "from the top to the base," maybe indicating the celestial cause of the event.

Its planning was noteworthy. Since this was the hour of the night yield, the ripping of the cloak couldn't have happened unnoticed. The hugeness of the opening of the Holy of Holies is put forward in Heb. 9:7,8; 10:19-22.

39. A "centurion" typically had one hundred men under his charge. In this occurrence, the officer was responsible for the littler separation

doled out to the execution. "Over against him." That is, he stood confronting the cross.

The centurion's assertion that Jesus "was the Son of God" should not be taken in the full Christian sense. In any case, the article does not show up in the Greek content. It ought to, in this manner, read "a Son of God" or no more, "God's Son." The agnostic foundation of the Roman officer must not be ignored. He may well have seen Jesus as a superhuman being; however, the fact that he had the full Christian idea of the deity of Christ is improbable. Besides, Luke records that he proclaimed Jesus to be "a righteous man" (23:47). For a commanding introduction of the inverse view, Lenski, Interpretation of Mark, pp.725-727.

40. "Mary Magdalene" is not to be mistaken for Mary of Bethany (Jn. 12:1 ff) nor with the wicked lady of Lk. 7:37. She originated from Magdala in Galilee, and she had encountered deliverance from evil spirit ownership (possession) at the order of Jesus (Lk. 8:2). The second "Mary" appears to have been the mother of James the child of Alphaeus, one of the pupils (Mk. 3:18). "Salome" is depicted as

the mother of James and John, the children of Zebedee (Matt. 27:56).

42. The record of the Passion closes with a depiction of the internment of Jesus (vv. 42-47). "The event" was come. The night alluded to here must have been early night, between the hour of the night yield (3:00 P.M.) and dusk (around 6:00 P.M.).

The game plans for entombment must be made before the start of "the sabbath" at twilight (cf. Jn. 19:31-17). Notice Mark's clarification of the Jewish expression, "the planning," for his Gentile perusers.

43. We don't know anything about "Josephy of Arimathaea" aside from what the Gospels exhibit regarding this occasion (cf. Matt. 27:57; Lk. 23:51; Jn. 19:38). "Hungered for." That is, he asked for (aiteo) the body.

46. The "fine cloth" was twisted around the assemblage of Jesus in strips (cf. Jn. 19:40, Greek content). The "catacomb" had been "slashed out" of shake by a stonecutter, a typical practice in that region. Matthew expresses that the tomb had a place with Joseph

and that it was new (27:60). The "stone" which was "moved" before the entryway was likely a level, roundabout chunk which came in a channel cut out of the stone for that purpose.

Chapter Sixteen

The Lord's Resurrection (16:1-20)

The last part of the Gospel falls into two unmistakably recognized areas. The visit of the three ladies to the tomb possesses 16:1-8. The rest of the part, 16:9-20, shapes a synopsis of the restoration appearances of Christ, finishing up with his climb.

1. Since "the sabbath" finished at nightfall, it gives the idea that the three ladies specified at 15:40 went to one of the shops that had been opened again for the night and obtained the coveted materials. The "sweet flavors" (aromata) were in a fluid shape; for example, they performed oil for the ladies who wanted to bless (anoint) the assortment of Jesus.

2. "Very Early." John says that it was as yet dark (20:1), though Mark expresses that it was "at the rising of the sun." The evident clash is effectively settled in the event that we expect that the women started their excursion while it was yet dark and touched base at the tomb soon after the sun had risen.

4. "When they looked." The word is anablepo, signifying "to look into." Perhaps as they

moved toward, they were strolling with bowed heads.

5. Mark reports that "they saw a young man." Matthew portrays the individual as a blessed messenger (angel) who had expelled the stone (28:2-4). What's more, Luke says there were two men in astonishing garments (24:4). The assortment is confirmation that these are the reports of a few observers, each of whom portrayed what awed her most.

The full story would incorporate the presence of two angels, one of whom rolled the stone away and addressed the women. "Alarmed." The word is all the more precisely deciphered as absolutely stunned. Lenski utilizes "utterly amazed" (1961).

6. "Be not affrighted." It ought to be rendered, and stop being completely flabbergasted. The holy messenger (angel) guaranteed them that Jesus had "risen" and left, in confirmation of which he pointed out "where they had laid him." John 20:6,7 advises us that the grave clothes (ASV) were still there in their place.

7. See how "Peter" is singled out in the course of action for a meeting in "Galilee." By that Christ had not rejected him, therefore of his disavowals (14:66-72).

Examination with alternate Gospels demonstrates that the followers did not leave on the double for Galilee and that Christ initially appeared to Peter (Lk. 24:34) and after that to the followers that night (Lk. 24:36). The meeting in Galilee is recorded in Matt. 28:16-20.

8. "They trembled and were amazed." Mark's uniqueness is significantly more grounded. He says, "....trembling and shock were holding them." It is no big surprise that they "fled from the sepulchre." The announcement that they don't say anything "to any man" must be comprehended in the light of alternate Gospels.

They don't say anything to anybody en route, for they are apprehensive and in a rush to take the news to the disciples (cf. Matt. 28:8; Lk. 24:9,10).

A Textual Note (16:9-20)

In the two most reliable original copies of the Greek NT (the Vaticanus and Sinaiticus), the Gospel closes with 16:8, as it does likewise in a few early forms. Both Eusebius and Jerome express that the closure was lost from a large portion of the original copies of their day.

What's more, a few writings and forms off a shorter substitute in the place of 16:9-20. By a wide margin, the more prominent number of original copies have the more extended conclusion; however, a considerable number of them are of a late date and of second-rate quality. By the perceived gauges of literary assessment, both the more drawn-out and shorter endings must be rejected, and this is the judgment of every single printed researcher.

Lenski is one of only a handful couple of commentators who contend for longer completion (Lenski, 1951). Likewise, an examination of verses 9-20 can't neglect to inspire the cautious understudy with the way that these verses contrast extraordinarily in style from whatever is left of the Gospel.

Maybe the most satisfactory clarification is that the finish of the first Gospel may have been detached and lost before extra duplicates could be made. Maybe others endeavored to supply a substitute closure, the best of which was what now shows up in 16:9-20.

9-11. The first record, which is here abridged, is to be found in Jn. 20:11-18. See the creator's accentuation on the unbelief of the followers (Mark 16:11,13,14).

12-13. For an entire record of this occasion, see Luke 24:13-35. "In another shape." Luke 24:16 says that their eyes were, in some way or another, influenced with the goal that they didn't perceive Christ. Regardless of whether Christ really changed his appearance, we don't have the foggiest idea. The "deposit" was the eleven disciples in Jerusalem (Lk. 24:33).

14-18. This appearance to "the eleven" took after instantly upon the report of the Emmaus explorers (Lk. 24:36-49; Jn. 20:19-25). Luke and John don't make the feeling that Jesus chastened them for "their unbelief and remorselessness"; however, he perceived how hard it was for them to accept, and he looked to expel their trouble by offering confirmations of his revival.

"He that believeth and is baptized through water." Some have utilized this verse to demonstrate that submersion is important for salvation. In any case, the way that the announcement seems just in this faulty conclusion to the book of Mark ought to demonstrate the requirement for alert in the utilization of the verse as proof content.

And afterward, it ought to be noticed that in the second 50% of the verse, the main reason for judgment is a refusal to accept. It might accordingly be reasoned that the main reason for salvation is conviction. Such an elucidation is in full agreement with the instructing of the NT all in all regarding the matter (cf. Rom. 3:28; Eph. 2:8,9).

This announcement concerning throwing out evil spirits (villains) and talking with new tongues (v.17) could well have a reference to events in the early church as recorded in Acts. Indeed, even the words about taking up "serpents" might be an inference to Paul's involvement in Acts 28:1-6.

The NT contains no other entry managing drinking poison ("any destructive thing"). Regardless of the possibility that this entry was irrefutably certified, it couldn't sensibly be utilized as a reason for the think and pretentious treatment of snakes and drinking of toxic substances, which are honed by certain outrageous religious (not Christian) factions.

The Final Summary (16:19-20)

This final summary is concerned with the ascension of Christ and the proceeding with the service of his devotees (followers). The expression, "after the Lord had talked," may appear to suggest that Christ's ascension happened promptly after his appearance to the eleven on the night of the day of his resurrection (vv. 14-18).

Nonetheless, an examination of Luke 24:50-53 and Acts 1:1-11 demonstrates that forty days had passed since his death. The end verse of the Gospel could well fill in as a short or extremely concise synopsis of the book of Acts. "The Lord

..... affirming the word." Note the striking likeness to Hebrews 2:4.

Bibliography

Alford, H. (1958) The Greek Testament.
Revised By Everett F. Harrison, Vol. I.
Chicago, Ill.: The Moody Press

Beasley-Murray, G.R. (1957) A Commentary
On Mark Thirteen. London, Eng.:
Macmillan & Company, Ltd

Branscomb, H. (1952) The Gospel Of Mark
(The Moffatt New Testament Commentary).
London, Eng.: Hodder & Stoughton, Ltd

Bruce, A.B. (n.d.) "The Synoptic Gospels."
The Expositor's Greek Testament,
Edited By W. Robertson Nicoll. Vol. I., Grand
Rapids, MI.: William B.
Eerdmans Publishing

Deissman, A. (1908) Light From The Ancient
East: The New Testament Illustrated by Recent
Discovered Texts Of The Graeco-Roman
World. Translated By R.M.

Strachan. New York, NY.: London, Eng.: Hodder & Stoughton

Gould, E.P. (1948, 2016) The Gospel According To St. Mark (The International Critical Commentary). Grand Rapids, MI.: Zondervan Publishing House,
Leopold Classic Library

Grant, F.C. & Luccock, H.E. (1951) "The Gospel According To St. Mark," The Interpreter's Bible, Vol. 7. New York, NY.: Abingdon – Cokesbury

Moldenke, H.N. & Moldenke, A. L. (1986) Plants Of The Bible. Mineola, NY.:
Dover Publications

Moore, G.F. (1997) Judaism In The First Three Centuries Of The Christian Era. Peabody, Mass.: Hendrickson Publishers

Moulton, J.H. & Milligan,G. (1995) The Vocabulary Of The Greek Testament.
Ada, MI.: Baker Academic, Bilingual Edition – Baker Publishing Group

Robertson, A.T. (1932, 1950) A Harmony Of The Gospels. (Reprint Edition) New York, NY.: Harper & Row

Swete, H. B. (1953) The Gospel According To St. Mark. London, Eng.: Mcmillian & Company, Ltd

Taylor. V. (1953) The Gospel According To Saint Mark. London, Eng.: Macmillian & Company, Ltd

The Holy Bible (1964) The Authorized King James Version. Chicago, Ill.: J.G. Ferguson Company

The Holy Bible (1901) The American Standard Version. Nashville, TN.: Thomas Nelson (used by permission)

The Holy Bible (1952) The Revised Standard Version. Nashville, TN.: Thomas Nelson & Sons (used by permission)

The New Combined Bible Dictionary And Concordance (1984) Dallas, TX.: Baker Book Company

About The Author

The Reverend Dr. John Thomas Wylie is one who has dedicated his life to the work of God's Service, the service of others, and being a powerful witness for the Gospel of Our Lord and Savior Jesus Christ. Dr. Wylie was called into the Gospel Ministry in June 1979, whereby in that same year he entered The American Baptist College of the American Baptist Theological Seminary, Nashville, Tennessee.

As a young seminarian, he read every book available to him that would help him better understand God, God's plan of salvation, and the Christian faith. He made a commitment as a promising student that he would inspire others as God inspires him. He understood early in his ministry that we live in times where people question not only who God is but also whether miracles are real, whether or not man can make a change, who the enemy is, or if the enemy truly exists.

Dr. Wylie carried out his commitment to God, which has been one of excellence which led to his earning his Bachelor of Arts in Bible/Theology/Pastoral Studies. Faithful and obedient to the call of God, he continued to matriculate in his studies earning his Master of Ministry from Emmanuel Bible College, Nashville, Tennessee & Emmanuel Bible College, Rossville, Georgia. Still, inspired to please the Lord and do that which is well-pleasing in the Lord's sight, Dr. Wylie recently on March 2006, completed his Masters of Education degree with a concentration in Instructional Technology earned at The American Intercontinental University, Holloman Estates, Illinois. Dr. Wylie also previous to this, earned his Education Specialist Degree from Jones International University, Centennial, Colorado and his Doctorate of Theology from The Holy Trinity College and Seminary, St. Petersburg, Florida.

Dr. Wylie has served in the capacity of pastor at two congregations in Middle Tennessee and Southern Tennessee, as well as served as an

Evangelistic Preacher, Teacher, Chaplain, Christian Educator, and finally, a published author and writer of many great inspirational Christian Publications, such as his first publication: "Only One God: Who Is He?" – published August 2002 via formal 1st books library (which is now AuthorHouse Book Publishers located in Bloomington, Indiana & Milton Keynes, United Kingdom) which caught the attention of The Atlanta Journal-Constitution Newspaper.

Dr. Wylie's present publication is in a series, "A Commentary On The Gospel Of Mark," by a God-fearing man who is not only an exceptional, prolific writer or inspiring himself but also Dr. Wylie is one of whom many of his peers think very highly of and is well sought after by his peers.

Finally, Dr. Wylie is recognized for his many great inspirational works in 2022's 75th Edition of Who's Who in America.

About The Book

In the event that we swing to Mark 10:45, we can, without much of a stretch, decide on Mark's question in composing his Gospel. For even the Son of man came not to be served unto, but rather to serve, and to give his life a payment for some. Unlike Matthew, Mark was not attempting to demonstrate certain announcements and predictions concerning Jesus.

His exclusive protest in composing was to educate plainly certain realities regarding Jesus, His deeds more particularly than His words. That Jesus is the Son of God, he demonstrates, not by pronouncing how He came to earth but rather by indicating what He finished amid His short time on this planet, how His coming changed the world.

There is a general understanding that Mark's Gospel was composed for Roman readers. The Romans were not quite the same as the Jews. His virtuoso was his solid judgment skills. His religion must be viable. He would have no enthusiasm for following convictions back into the past. Lawful family histories and achievements of prescience would abandon him frosty. Jewish doctrines were not in his line.

He may state, "I don't know anything of your Scriptures, and watch over your impossible to miss ideas; yet I ought to be happy to hear a plain story of the life this man Jesus lived. Reveal to me what He did. Give me a chance to see Him similarly as He seemed to be.

Mark varies broadly from Matthew in both character and extension. Mark's Gospel is the most brief of them all. Matthew has twenty-eight chapters, possesses large amounts of illustrations, and depicts Christ as the Son of David with royal kingly dignity and authority (Matthew 28:18).

Mark has sixteen chapters and gives four stories. Mark depicts Christ as the humble but Perfect Servant of Jehovah (God). We discover the blessed messengers (angels) serving unto Him.

www.ingramcontent.com/pod-product-compliance
Lightning Source LLC
LaVergne TN
LVHW040140080526
838202LV00042B/2964